# Doré's Illustrations for
# "IDYLLS OF THE KING"

GUSTAVE DORÉ

DOVER PUBLICATIONS, INC.
New York

## *Copyright*



Published in Canada by General Publishing Company, Ltd., 30 Lesmill Road, Don Mills, Toronto, Ontario.
Published in the United Kingdom by Constable and Company, Ltd., 3 The Lanchesters, 162–164 Fulham Palace Road, London W6 9ER.

## *Bibliographical Note*

This Dover edition, first published in 1995, reproduces all 36 plates from the following volumes (9 plates in each volume); *Guinevere*, by Alfred Tennyson, illustrated by Gustave Doré (London: Edward Moxon and Co., 1867); *Vivien*, by Alfred Tennyson, illustrated by Gustave Doré (London: Edward Moxon and Co., 1867); *Elaine*, by Alfred Tennyson, illustrated by Gustave Doré (London: Edward Moxon and Co., 1868); and *Enid*, by Alfred Tennyson, illustrated by Gustave Doré (London: E. Moxon, Son, and Co., 1869). The plates for this edition have been grouped according to the order of the original publication dates of Tennyson's four *Idylls* (see Note for additional bibliographical information). An introductory Note and summaries of the four *Idylls* have been specially prepared for this edition; excerpts of Tennyson's poetry are taken from the volumes listed above.

## DOVER *Pictorial Archive* SERIES



## *Library of Congress Cataloging-in-Publication Data*

Doré, Gustave, 1832–1883.
Doré's illustrations for "Idylls of the King" / Gustave Doré.— Dover ed.
p. cm. — (Dover pictorial archives)
ISBN 0-486-28465-4 (pbk.)
1. Doré, Gustave, 1832–1883—Themes, motives. 2. Tennyson, Alfred Tennyson, Baron, 1809–1892. Idylls of the King.—Illustrations. I. Title. II. Series: Dover pictorial archive series.
NE650.D646A4 1995
769.92—dc20 95-16565
CIP

Manufactured in the United States of America
Dover Publications, Inc., 31 East 2nd Street, Mineola, N.Y. 11501

# NOTE

GUSTAVE DORÉ WAS born in Strasbourg, France, on January 6, 1832. Early on Doré displayed his artistic talents, and when he was 15, he began to exhibit his landscape sketches in pen-and-ink at the Paris Salon. That same year, 1848, he began contributing lithographic caricatures to the *Journal pour rire*. Though Doré never fulfilled his ambition to achieve fame as a historical painter, his wood-engraved book illustrations gained him a worldwide reputation. Doré's first such success came with the illustrations he produced for an edition of Rabelais in 1854. These were followed by an edition of Balzac's *Les Contes drolatiques* (1856). Other classics illustrated by Doré include Dante's *Inferno* (1861), *Perrault's Fairy Tales* (1861), Cervantes' *Don Quixote* (1863), Milton's *Paradise Lost* (1866) and Coleridge's *Rime of the Ancient Mariner* (1876). Doré died in Paris in 1883.

Alfred, Lord Tennyson (1809–1892), is considered by many to be the poetic voice of Victorian England. In 1850, *In Memoriam* ensured Tennyson's fame during his lifetime and Queen Victoria appointed him poet laureate that same year. *Idylls of the King*, first published in 1859, originally contained four of Tennyson's Arthurian poems—*Enid, Vivien, Elaine* and *Guinevere*. Over the next 25 years, Tennyson revised his original idylls extensively, completing the cycle in 1885 with *Balin and Balan*. In 1888 the *Idylls* were arranged in their final order (original publication dates in parentheses): *Dedication* (1862), *The Coming of Arthur* (1869), *Gareth and Lynette* (1872), *The Marriage of Geraint* (1857), *Geraint and Enid* (1857), *Balin and Balan* (1885), *Merlin and Vivien* (1857), *Lancelot and Elaine* (1859), *The Holy Grail* (1869), *Pelleas and Ettarre* (1869), *The Last Tournament* (1871), *Guinevere* (1859), *The Passing of Arthur* (1842) and *To the Queen* (1872).

# CONTENTS

*Enid* 2
*Vivien* 20
*Elaine* 38
*Guinevere* 56

# LIST OF PLATES

I. Yniol Shows Prince Geraint His Ruined Castle. 3
II. Enid and the Countess. 5
III. Edyrn with His Lady and Dwarf Journey to Arthur's Court. 7
IV. Geraint Charges the Bandits. 9
V. Geraint and Enid in the Meadow. 11
VI. The Flight of the Boon Companions of Earl Limours. 13
VII. Enid Tends Geraint. 15
VIII. Geraint Slays Earl Doorm. 17
IX. Geraint and Enid Ride Away. 19
X. Vivien and Merlin Repose. 21
XI. Vivien and Merlin Disembark. 23
XII. Vivien and Merlin Enter the Woods. 25
XIII. The Knights' Carouse. 27
XIV. The Knights' Progress. 29
XV. Merlin Paints the Young Knight's Shield. 31
XVI. The Sea Fight. 33
XVII. The Cave Scene. 35
XVIII. Vivien Encloses Merlin in the Tree. 37
XIX. King Arthur Discovering the Skeletons of the Brothers. 39
XX. Lancelot Approaching the Castle of Astolat. 41
XXI. Lancelot Relating His Adventures. 43
XXII. Lancelot Bids Adieu to Elaine. 45
XXIII. Elaine on Her Road to the Cave of Lancelot. 47
XXIV. Torre and Lavaine Bid Farewell to the Body of Elaine. 49
XXV. The Body of Elaine on Its Way to King Arthur's Palace. 51
XXVI. King Arthur Reading the Letter of Elaine. 53
XXVII. The Remorse of Lancelot. 55
XXVIII. The Parting. 57
XXIX. The Moonlight Ride. 59
XXX. Cloister Scene. 61
XXXI. Terrace Scene. 63
XXXII. The Joyous Spirits. 65
XXXIII. The Fairy-Circle. 67
XXXIV. The Finding of King Arthur. 69
XXXV. The Dawn of Love. 71
XXXVI. The King's Farewell. 73

# Doré's Illustrations for "IDYLLS OF THE KING"

# ENID

## Plate I

Enid has been married to Prince Geraint—one of Arthur's knights of the Round Table—for a year, and at court, Enid is one of Queen Guinevere's favorites. Afraid that his wife might be influenced by Guinevere's adulterous behavior, Geraint takes her away from Camelot. Once they return to his own earldom, which has become lawless in his absence, Geraint becomes so obsessed with watching over Enid that he forgets all other duties, and is ridiculed by his own subjects. Enid feels she should say something to him, but cannot. One morning, as she watches Geraint sleeping, she begins to upbraid herself for not speaking frankly to her husband. He wakes, only to hear her last words: "O me, I fear that I am no true wife." Assuming his wife has been unfaithful, he determines to "ride forth into the wilderness" accompanied by Enid, who is to put on "her worst and meanest dress" as a sign of her offense. As she prepares to leave, ignorant of what she has done wrong, Enid recalls her first meeting with Geraint.

A year earlier, while Geraint is attending the Queen at a royal hunt, they see a strange knight, accompanied by a dwarf and a lady, ride by. Curious, the Queen asks Geraint to find out his name. When the knight refuses to answer, thereby insulting Geraint and the Queen, Geraint follows him to avenge the insult. Geraint's search leads him to the ruined castle of Yniol, Enid's father, who invites Geraint to partake of his hospitality. As Yniol escorts Geraint through the courtyard,

> He look'd and saw that all was ruinous.
> Here stood a shatter'd archway plumed with fern;
> And here had fall'n a great part of a tower,
> Whole, like a crag that tumbles from the cliff,
> And high above a piece of turret stair,
> Worn by the feet that now were silent, wound
> Bare to the sun, and monstrous ivy-stems
> Claspt the gray walls with hairy-fibred arms,
> And suck'd the joining of the stones, and look'd
> A knot, beneath, of snakes, aloft, a grove. (315–325)

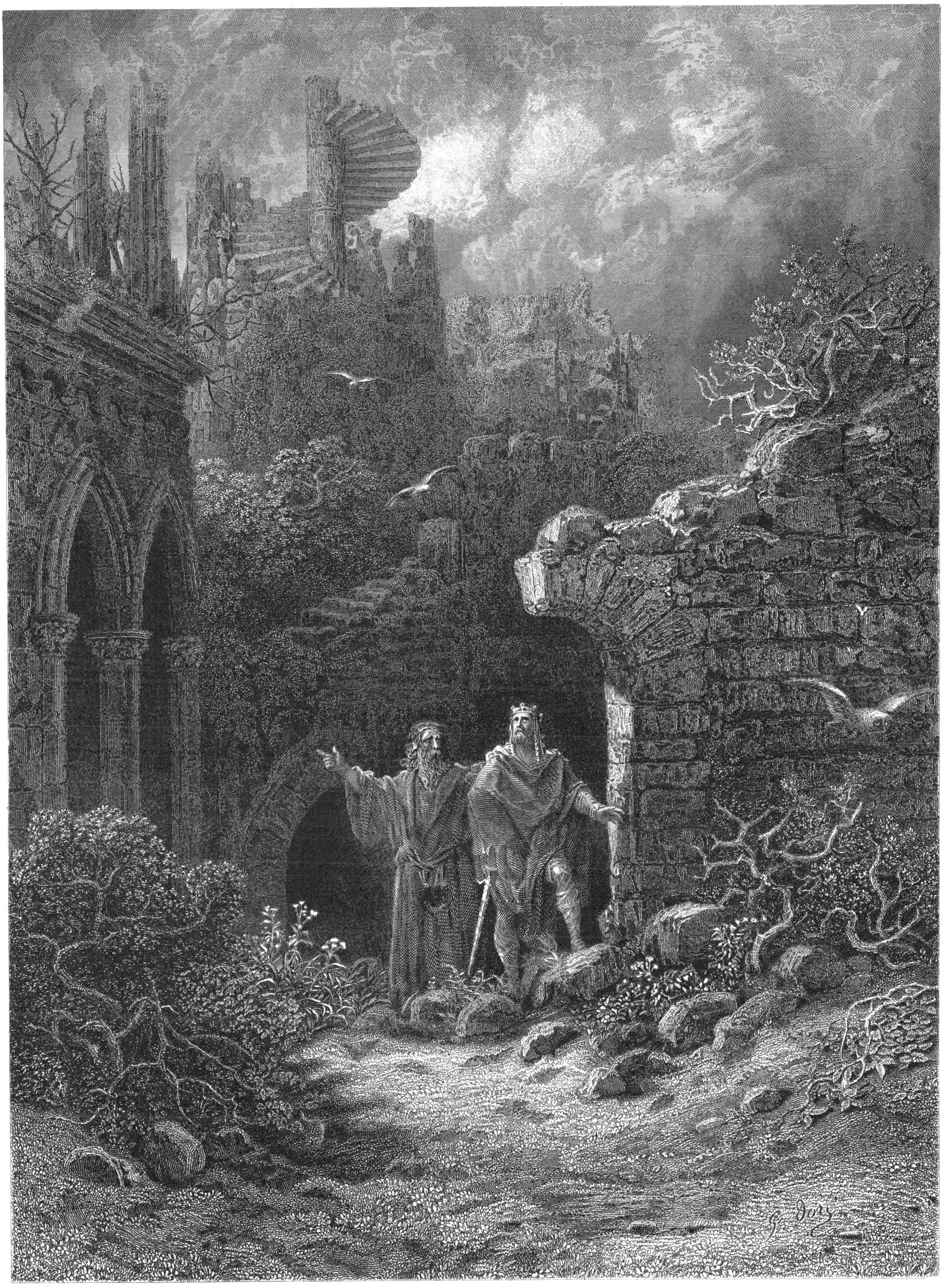

# Plate II

Geraint is served that evening by Enid, who must assume the role of servant because her family is so poor. First attracted by her beauty, Geraint is further charmed at "seeing her so sweet and serviceable," and before the evening is through he falls in love with her. Meanwhile Yniol tells Geraint that the knight he seeks is his own nephew, known as the "sparrow-hawk." This knight, once Enid's suitor, had been rejected by Yniol; infuriated, he brought Yniol's family to ruin and usurped Yniol's earldom. Geraint, on hearing the story, offers to challenge the sparrow-hawk at the tournament to be held the following day. Although he appreciates Geraint's offer, Yniol explains that no man can tilt, "Except the lady he loves best be there." Geraint then reveals that he loves Enid and, with Yniol's permission, he will fight the sparrow-hawk and claim victory in her name. Yniol agrees and sends his wife to tell Enid, who doesn't respond with words, but is clearly honored by Geraint's favor:

Nor did she lift an eye nor speak a word,
Rapt in the fear and in the wonder of it;
So moving without answer to her rest
She found no rest, and ever fail'd to draw
The quiet night into her blood, but lay
Contemplating her own unworthiness;
And when the pale and bloodless east began
To quicken to the sun, arose, and raised
Her mother too, and hand in hand they moved
Down to the meadow where the jousts were held,
And waited there for Yniol and Geraint.
  And thither came the twain, and when Geraint
Beheld her first in field, awaiting him,
He felt, were she the prize of bodily force,
Himself beyond the rest could move
The chair of Idris. (528–543)

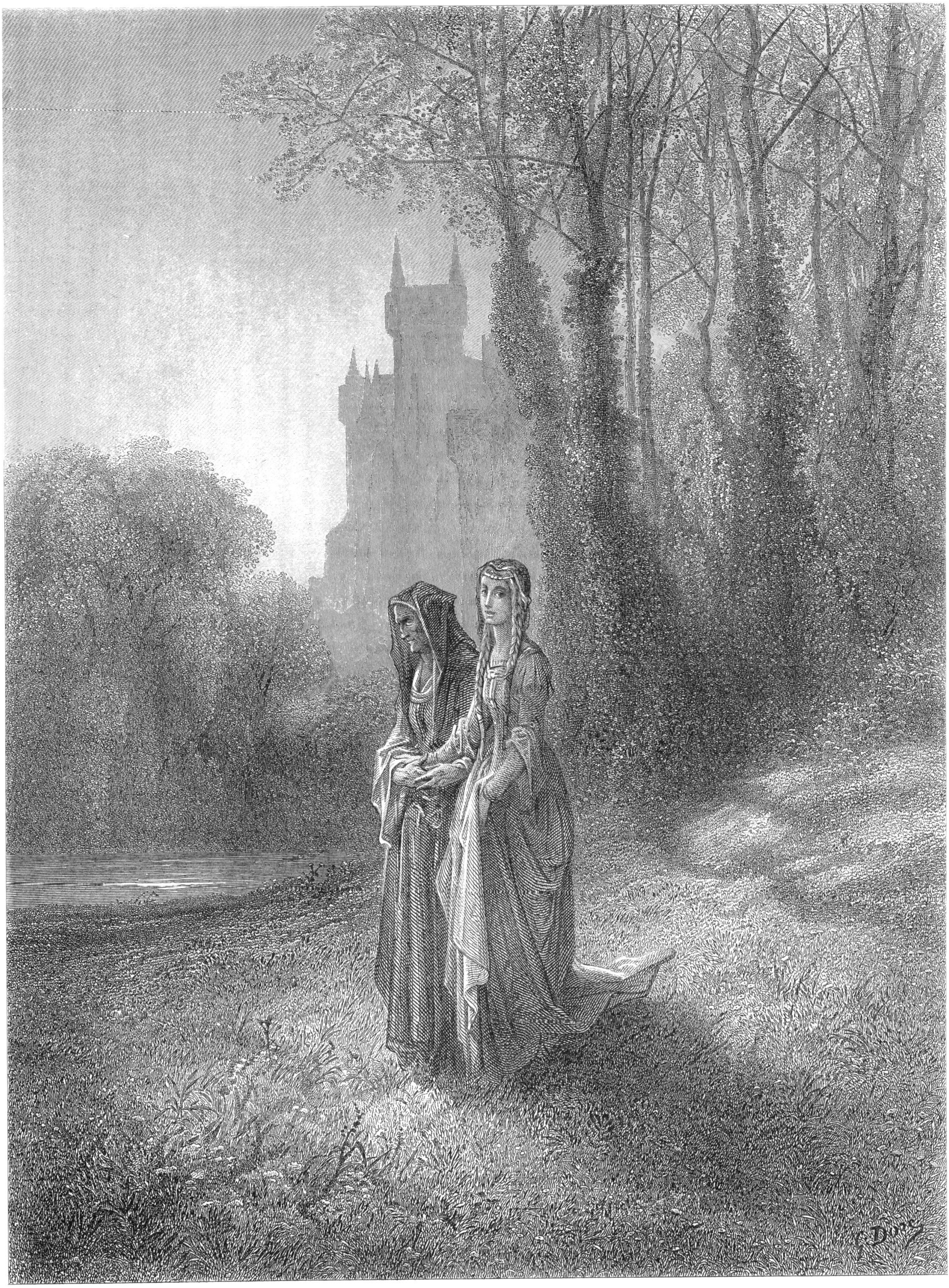

## Plate III

Soon the tournament grounds are filled with knights and ladies, and the field is prepared: "Two forks are fix't into the meadow ground, / And over these is laid a silver wand, / And over that is placed the sparrow-hawk, / The prize of beauty for the fairest there." For the past two years, Yniol's nephew has won the prize, and so won the name "sparrow-hawk." As he claims the prize—not expecting any challengers—Geraint boldly comes forward. The two men are evenly matched, and the battle is fierce; just when both are nearly exhausted, Yniol cries to Geraint, "Remember that great insult done the Queen." Inspired, Geraint conquers the sparrow-hawk and once again asks his name.

[T]he fallen man
Made answer, groaning, "Edyrn, son of Nudd!
Ashamed am I that I should tell it thee.
My pride is broken: men have seen my fall."
"Then, Edyrn, son of Nudd," replied Geraint,
"These two things shalt thou do, or else thou diest.
First, thou thyself, thy lady, and thy dwarf,
Shalt ride to Arthur's court, and being there,
Crave pardon for that insult done the Queen,
And shalt abide her judgment on it; next,
Thou shalt give back their earldom to thy kin.
These two things shalt thou do, or thou shalt die."
And Edyrn answer'd, "These things will I do,
For I have never yet been overthrown,
And thou hast overthrown me, and my pride
Is broken down, for Enid sees my fall!"
And rising up, he rode to Arthur's court,
And there the Queen forgave him easily. (575–592)

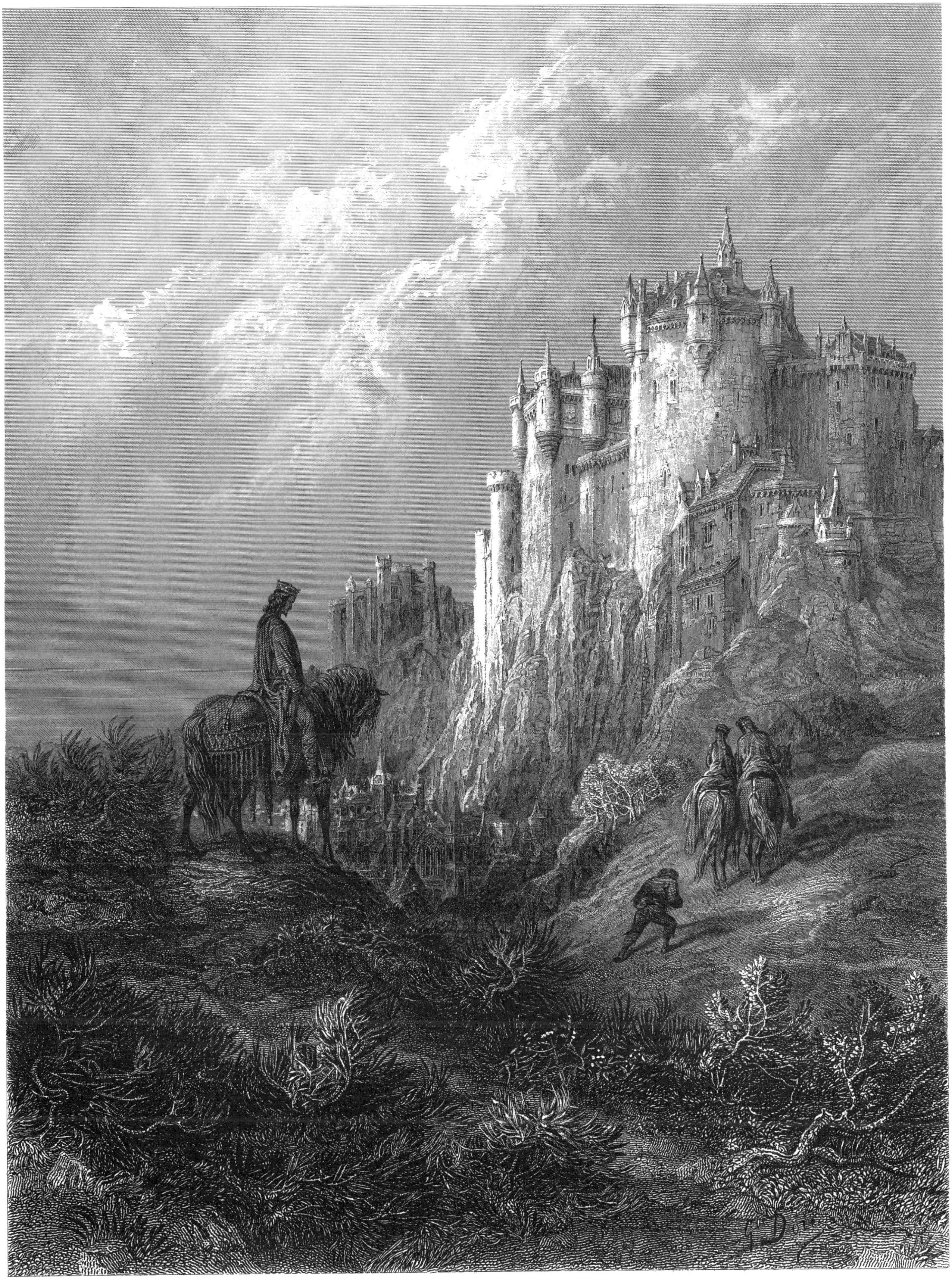

# Plate IV

Enid and Geraint travel to Camelot after the tournament, where they are married "with all ceremony." Now, a year later, the two prepare for another journey. Geraint orders Enid to ride ahead of him—not by his side—and charges her, whatever happens, not to speak to him. As they travel, past "bandit-haunted holds, / Gray swamps and pools, waste places of the hern, / And wildernesses, perilous paths," Enid notices three knights, "caitiffs all," lying in wait for them. Despite Geraint's command, Enid turns back to warn her husband. Angry that she has disobeyed, Geraint prepares to prove to her that his "vigour is not lost." He conquers the villains, and claims as his prize their armor and horses, which he orders Enid to herd before her. They move on, and once more Enid spies three horsemen waiting to ambush them. She turns back again to warn Geraint:

"There lurk three villains yonder in the wood,
And each of them is wholly arm'd, and one
Is larger-limb'd than you are, and they say
That they will fall upon you while you pass."
   To which he flung a wrathful answer back:
"And if there were an hundred in the wood,
And every man were larger-limb'd than I,
And all at once should sally out upon me,
I swear it would not ruffle me so much
As you that not obey me. Stand aside,
And if I fall, cleave to the better man."
   And Enid stood aside to wait the event,
Not dare to watch the combat, only breathe
Short fits of prayer, at every stroke a breath.
And he, she dreaded most, bare down upon him.
Aim'd at the helm, his lance err'd; but Geraint's,
A little in the late encounter strain'd
Struck thro' the bulky bandit's corselet home,
And then brake short, and down his enemy roll'd,
And there lay still. (991–1010)

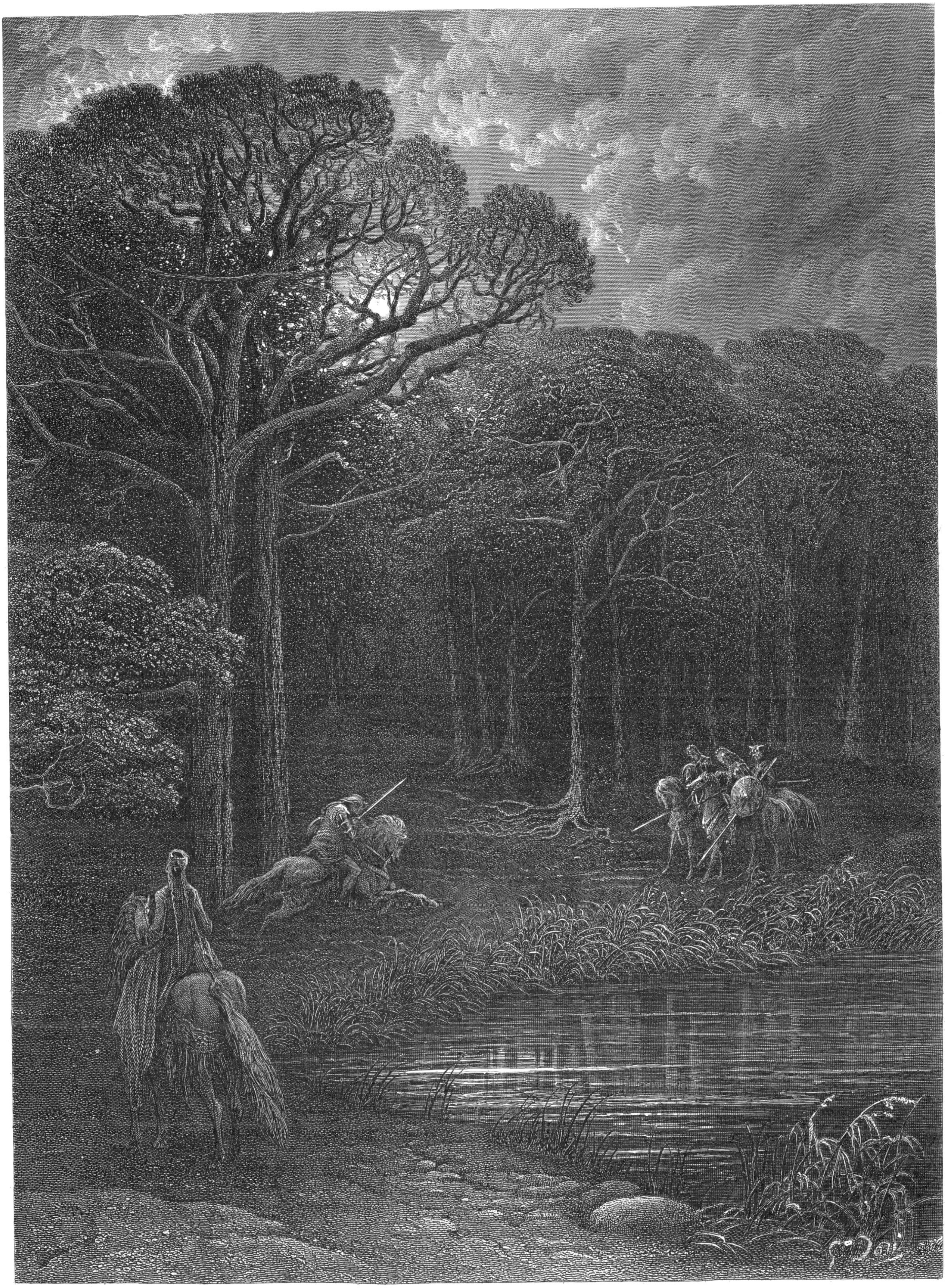

# Plate V

After defeating these bandits, Geraint takes their horses and armor as well, and gives them with the others to Enid to herd along.

So thro' the green gloom of the wood they past,  
And issuing under open heavens beheld  
A little town with towers, upon a rock,  
And close beneath, a meadow gemlike chased  
In the brown wild, and mowers mowing in it:  
And down a rocky pathway from the place  
There came a fair-hair'd youth, that in his hand  
Bare victual for the mowers: and Geraint  
Had ruth again on Enid looking pale:  
Then, moving downward to the meadow ground,  
He, when the fair-hair'd youth came by him, said,  
"Friend, let her eat; the damsel is so faint."  
"Yea, willingly," replied the youth; "and you,  
My lord, eat also, tho' the fare is coarse,  
And only meet for mowers;" then set down  
His basket, and dismounting on the sward  
They let the horses graze, and ate themselves. (1044–1060)

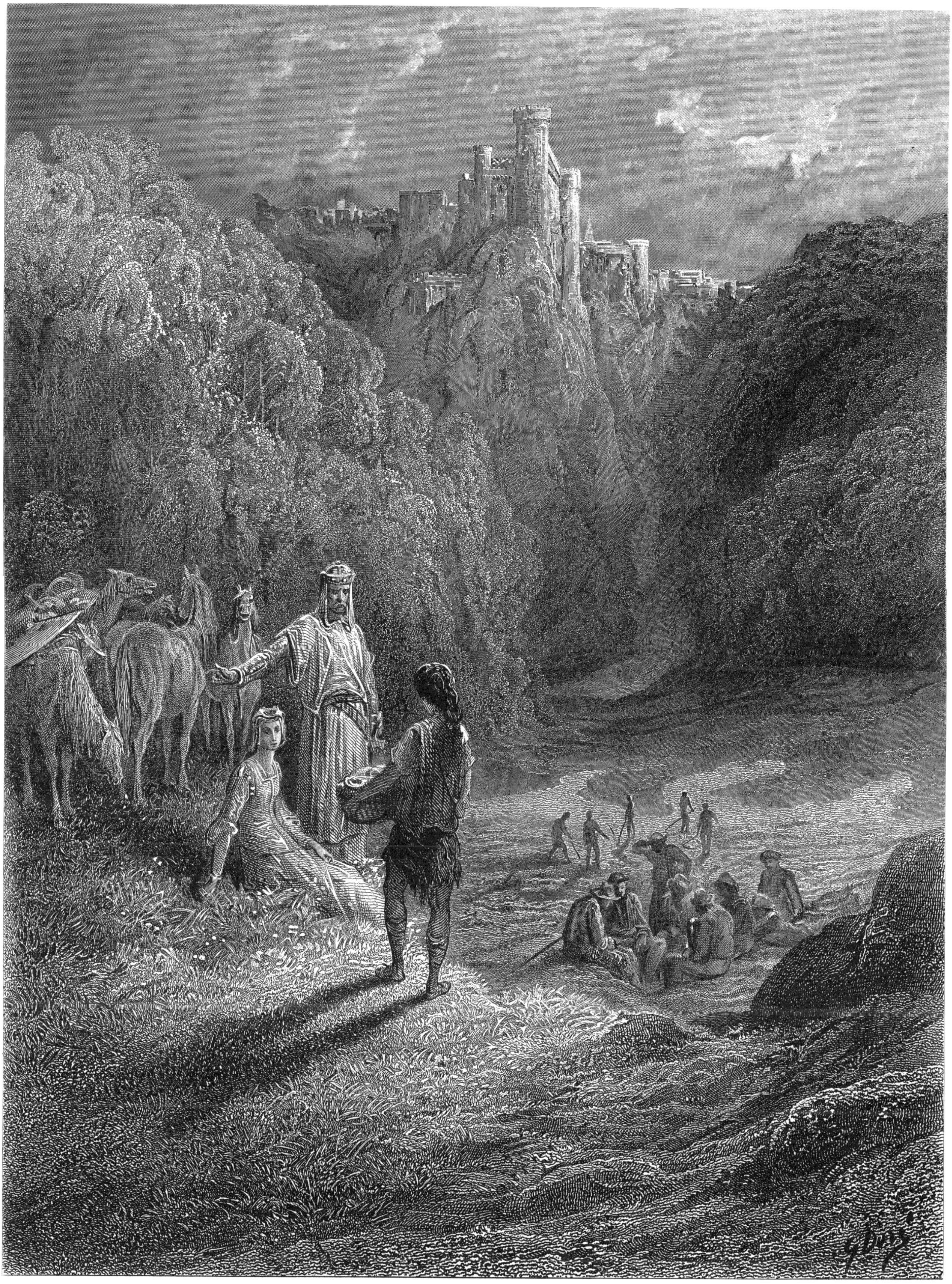

# Plate VI

THE YOUTH THEN leads the couple to lodging for the night. They are waked by a loud party of revelers, led by Limours, "the wild lord of the place." In years past, Limours was also a suitor of Enid, and seeing her again rekindles his ardour. At the first opportunity he speaks to her alone and tries to convince her to leave Geraint. Limours points out that her husband cannot love her, as proved by her "wretched dress, / A wretched insult" on her. Enid listens to Limours' plot to kill Geraint so they can be reunited and, pretending to agree, she claims exhaustion and tells him to return in the morning to fulfill his plans. Early the next day, as Geraint sleeps, Enid prepares his armor "All to be there against a sudden need." He wakes and Enid tells him that Limours will be there soon. She helps Geraint arm himself, and the two leave, Geraint once again commanding Enid to remain silent. They have not traveled far when Enid looks back to see Limours and his companions following them. She remains silent, but warns Geraint by pointing to the pursuers.

> At which the warrior in his obstinacy,
> Because she kept the letter of his word
> Was in a manner pleased, and turning, stood.
> And in the moment after, wild Limours,
> Borne on a black horse, like a thunder-cloud . . .
> Dash'd on Geraint, who closed with him, and bore
> Down by the length of lance and arm beyond
> The crupper, and so left him stunn'd or dead,
> And overthrew the next that follow'd him,
> And blindly rush'd on all the rout behind.
> But at the flash and motion of the man
> They vanish'd panic-stricken, like a shoal
> Of darting fish. (1303–1318)

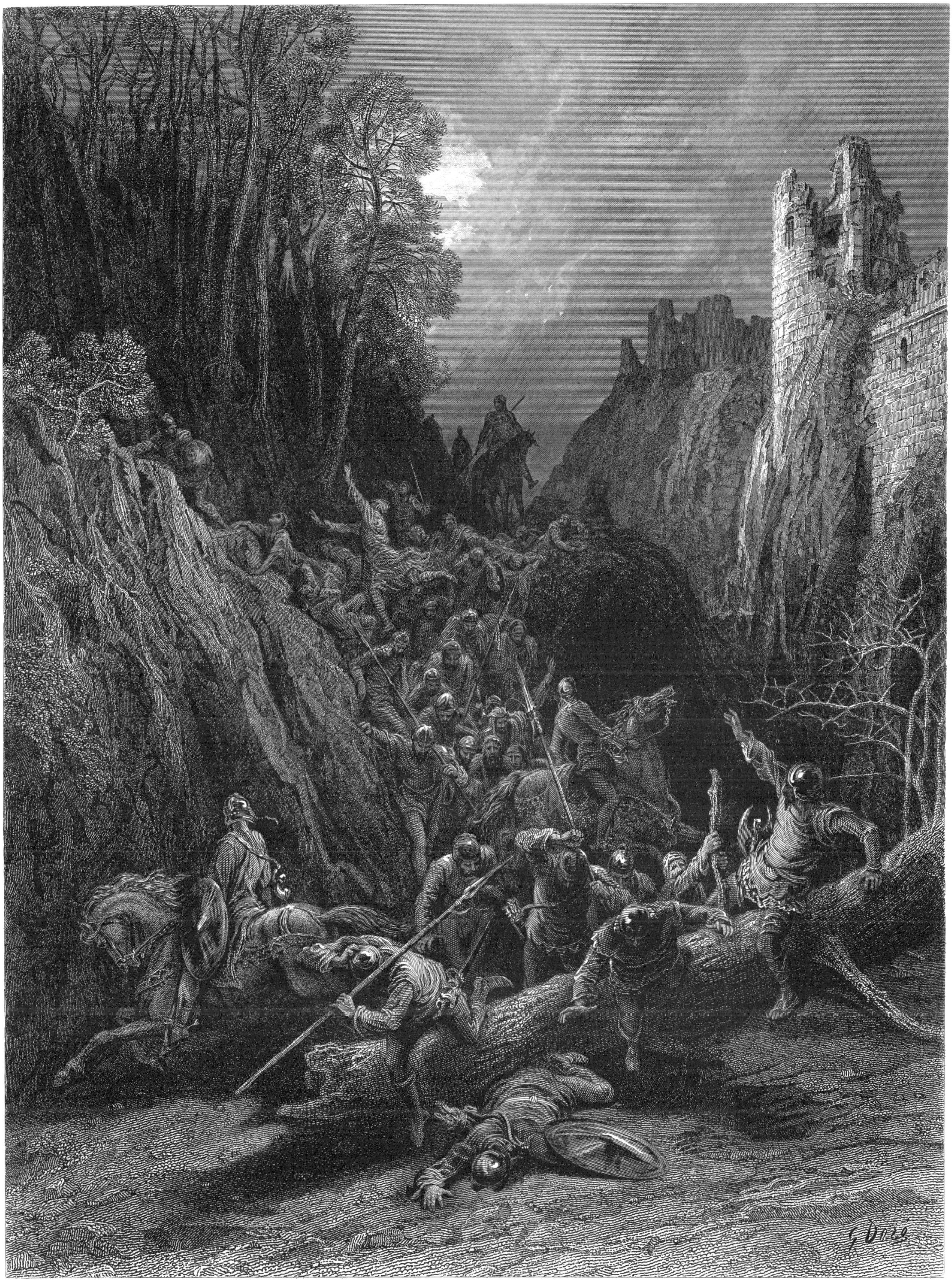

# Plate VII

Although Enid's warning has enabled Geraint to vanquish Limours, he remains unconvinced of his wife's fidelity. Geraint orders her to proceed on, "To the waste earldom of another earl, / Doorm, whom his shaking vassals call'd the Bull." Enid obeys, unaware that Geraint has been wounded until he falls from his horse.

And Enid heard the clashing of his fall,
Suddenly came, and at his side all pale
Dismounting, loosed the fastenings of his arms,
Nor let her true hand falter, nor blue eye
Moisten, till she had lighted on his wound,
And tearing off her veil of faded silk
Had bared her forehead to the blistering sun,
And swathed the hurt that drain'd her dear lord's life.
Then after all was done that hand could do,
She rested, and her desolation came
Upon her, and she wept beside the way.
And many past, but none regarded her,
For in that realm of lawless turbulence,
A woman weeping for her murder'd mate
Was cared as much for as a summer shower:
One took him for a victim of Earl Doorm,
Nor dared to waste a perilous pity on him:
Another hurrying past, a man-at-arms,
Rode on a mission to the bandit Earl;
Half whistling and half singing a coarse song,
He drove the dust against her veilless eyes:
Another, flying from the wrath of Doorm
Before an ever-fancied arrow, made
The long way smoke beneath him in his fear;
At which her palfrey whinnying lifted heel,
And scour'd into the coppices and was lost,
While the great charger stood, grieved like a man. (1358–1384)

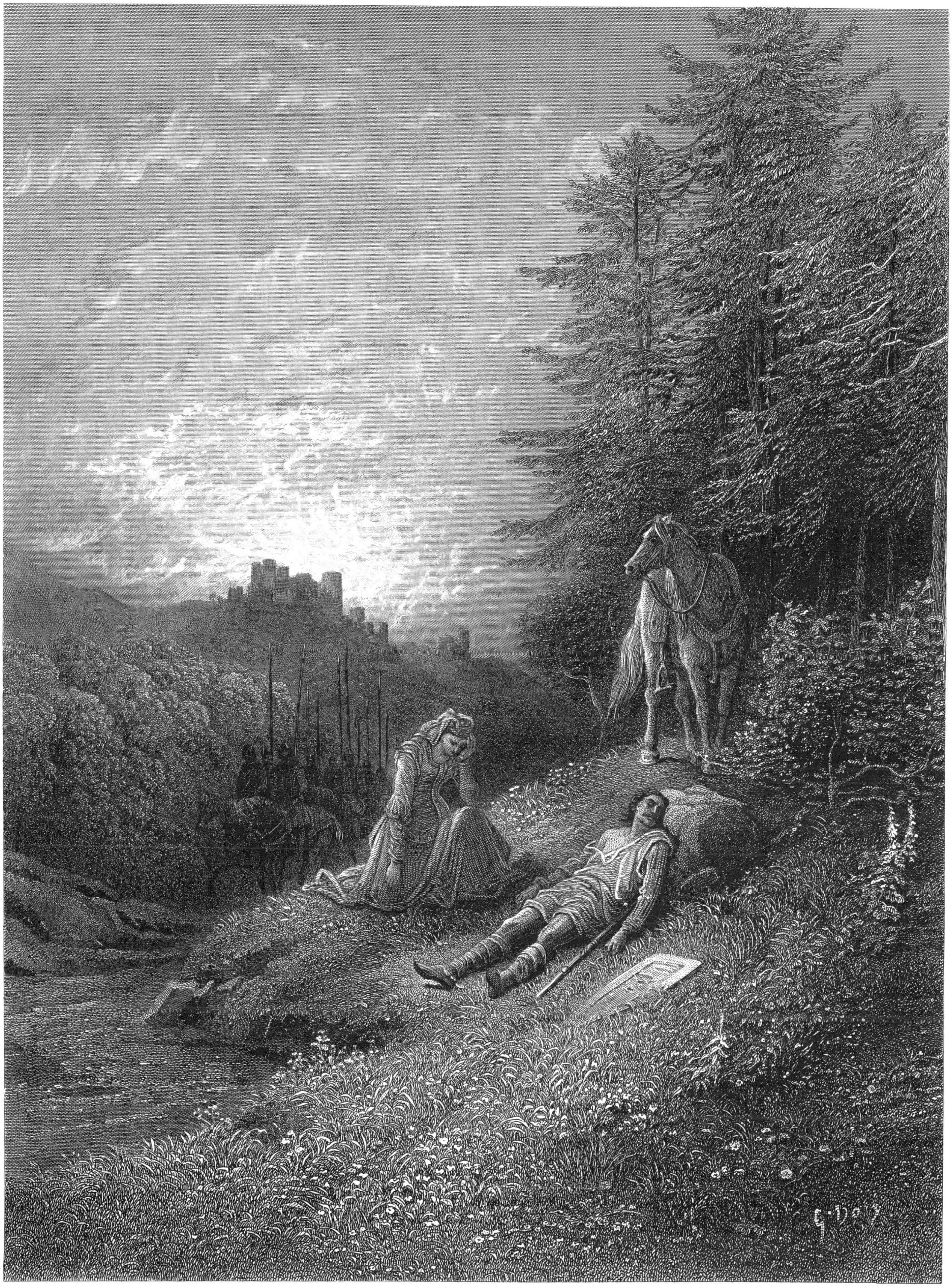

# Plate VIII

As Enid continues weeping at Geraint's side, "the huge Earl Doorm" comes riding past. He chides Enid for weeping over a dead man, or one as good as dead, and orders two of his men to take the couple to his hall. While Doorm and his men are out on a raid, Enid remains with Geraint, tending him until he regains consciousness. Believing at last that she loves him, he nevertheless "feigned himself as dead, / That he might prove her to the uttermost." Soon Doorm returns from his foray, and there is a great and noisy banquet. "To shun the wild ways of the lawless tribe," Enid tries to shrink back from view. The earl sees her, and angry that she still grieves over Geraint—who he assumes is dead—he commands her to come eat and drink. Enid repeatedly refuses Doorm's orders and calls upon his "gentleness" to leave her alone.

   Then strode the brute Earl up and down his hall,
And took his russet beard between his teeth;
Last, coming up quite close, and in his mood
Crying, "I count it of no more avail,
Dame, to be gentle than ungentle with you;
Take my salute," unknightly with flat hand,
However lightly, smote her on the cheek.
   Then Enid, in her utter helplessness,
And since she thought, "he had not dared to do it,
Except he surely knew my lord was dead,"
Sent forth a sudden sharp and bitter cry,
As of a wild thing taken in the trap,
Which sees the trapper coming thro' the wood.
   This heard Geraint, and grasping at his sword . . .
Made but a single bound, and with a sweep of it
Shore thro' the swarthy neck, and like a ball
The russet-bearded head roll'd on the floor.
So died Earl Doorm by him he counted dead. (1561–1579)

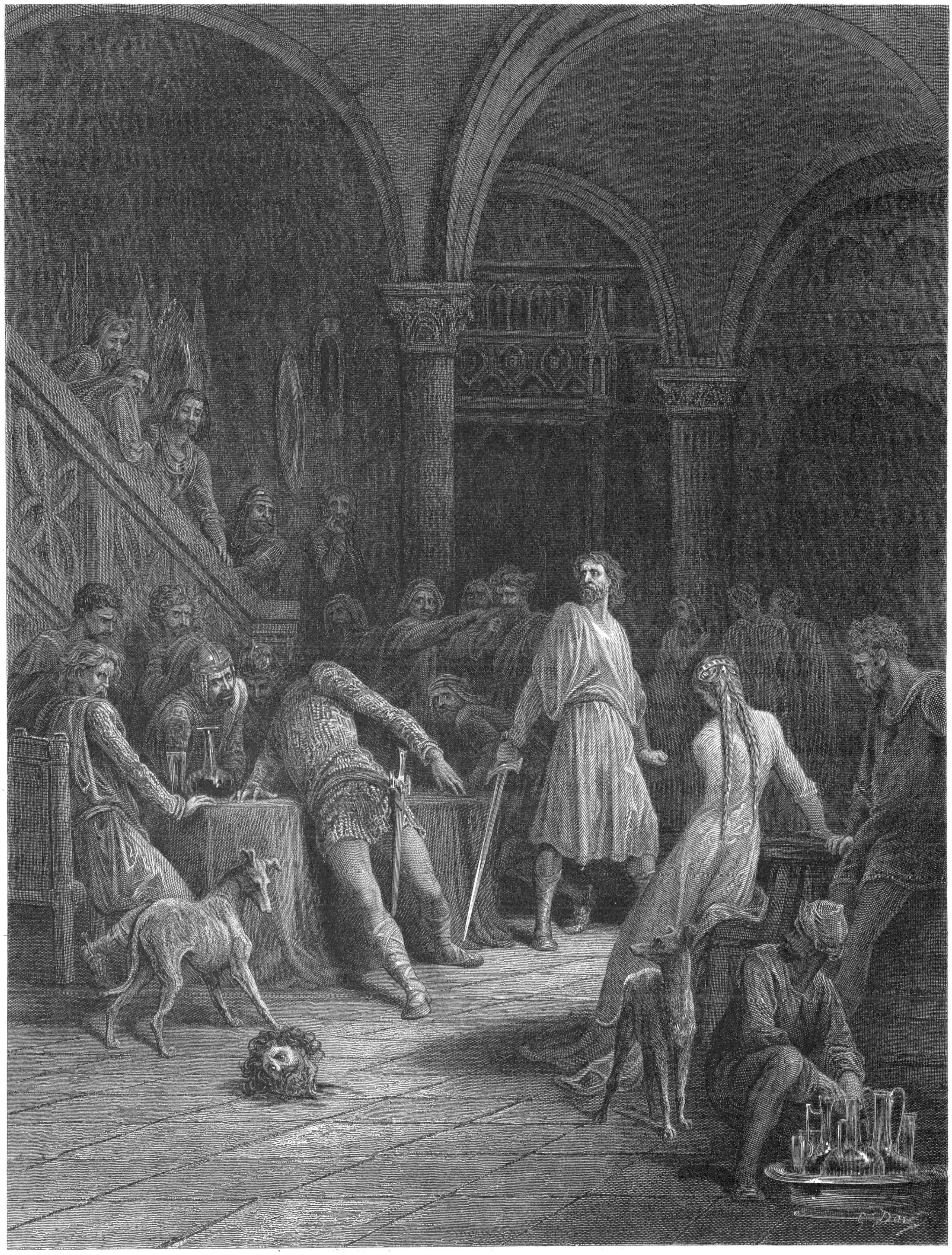
G. Doré

# Plate IX

After Geraint kills Doorm, the earl's followers flee. Geraint begs Enid's forgiveness, admitting his wrongs and confessing he had overheard her say she was untrue. Enid, still worried that Doorm's men will return, can only respond by urging him to leave. Outside the hall, they find Geraint's charger waiting.

[T]hen Geraint upon the horse
Mounted, and reach'd a hand, and on his foot
She set her own and climb'd; he turn'd his face
And kiss'd her climbing, and she cast her arms
About him, and at once they rode away.
And never yet, since high in Paradise
O'er the four rivers the first roses blew,
Came purer pleasure unto mortal kind
Than lived thro' her, who in that perilous hour
Put hand to hand beneath her husband's heart,
And felt him hers again. . . .
[A]nd in their halls arose
The cry of children, Enids and Geraints
Of times to be; nor did he doubt her more
But rested in her fëalty, till he crown'd
A happy life with a fair death, and fell
Against the heathen of the Northern Sea
In battle, fighting for the blameless King. (1607–1819)

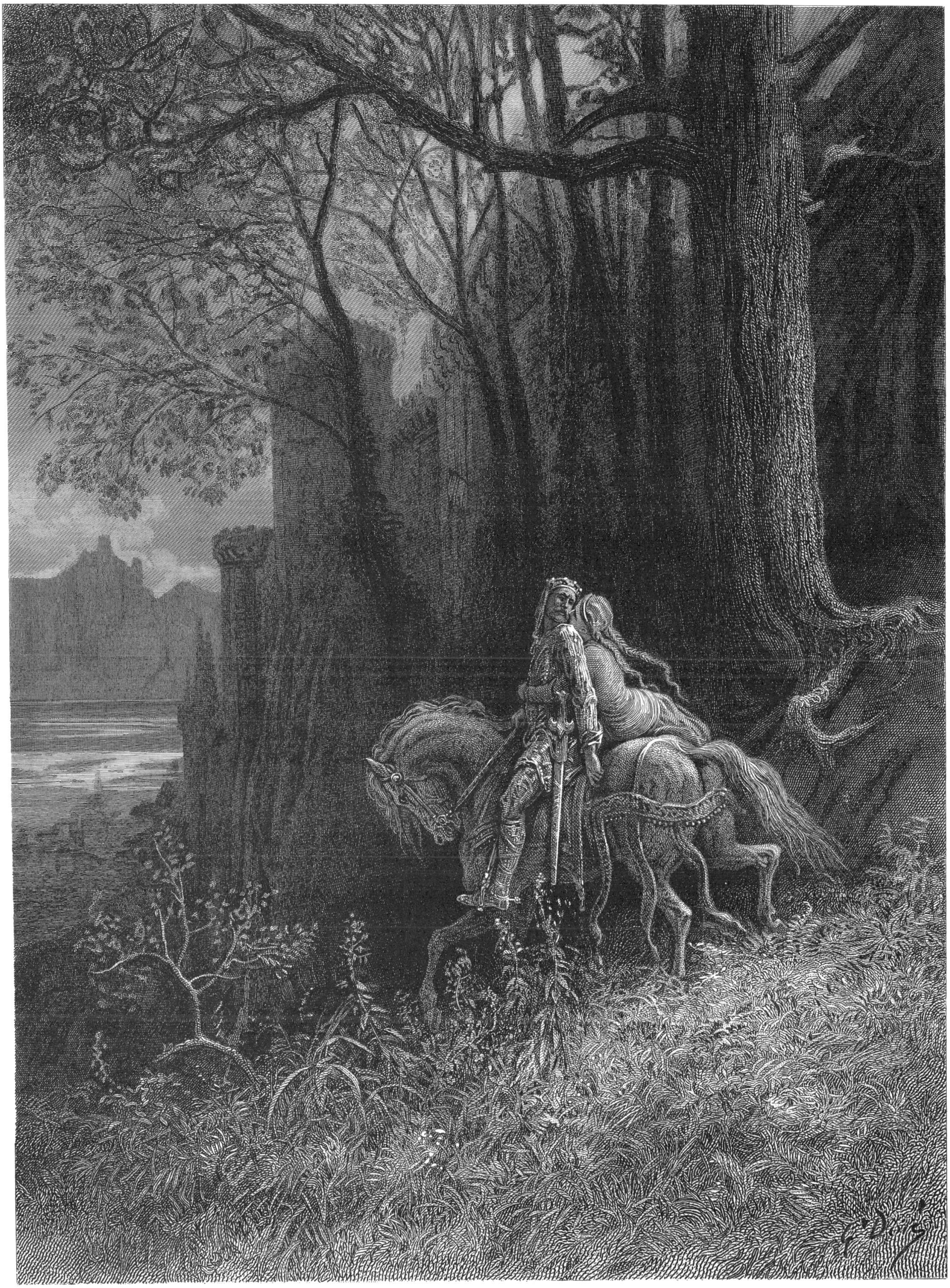

# VIVIEN

## Plate X

*Vivien* presents the romance of the famous magician of Camelot and the enchantress who brings about his ruin. Merlin, now an old man, has left Camelot, suffering from "a great melancholy," and Vivien has followed him.

A storm was coming, but the winds were still
And in the wild woods of Broceliande,
Before an oak, so hollow huge and old
It look'd a tower of ruin'd masonwork,
At Merlin's feet the wily Vivien lay. . . .
   There she lay all her length and kiss'd his feet,
As if in deepest reverence and in love.
A twist of gold was round her hair; a robe
Of samite without price, that more exprest
Than hid her, clung about her lissome limbs,
In colour like the satin-shining palm
On sallows in the windy gleams of March. (1–74)

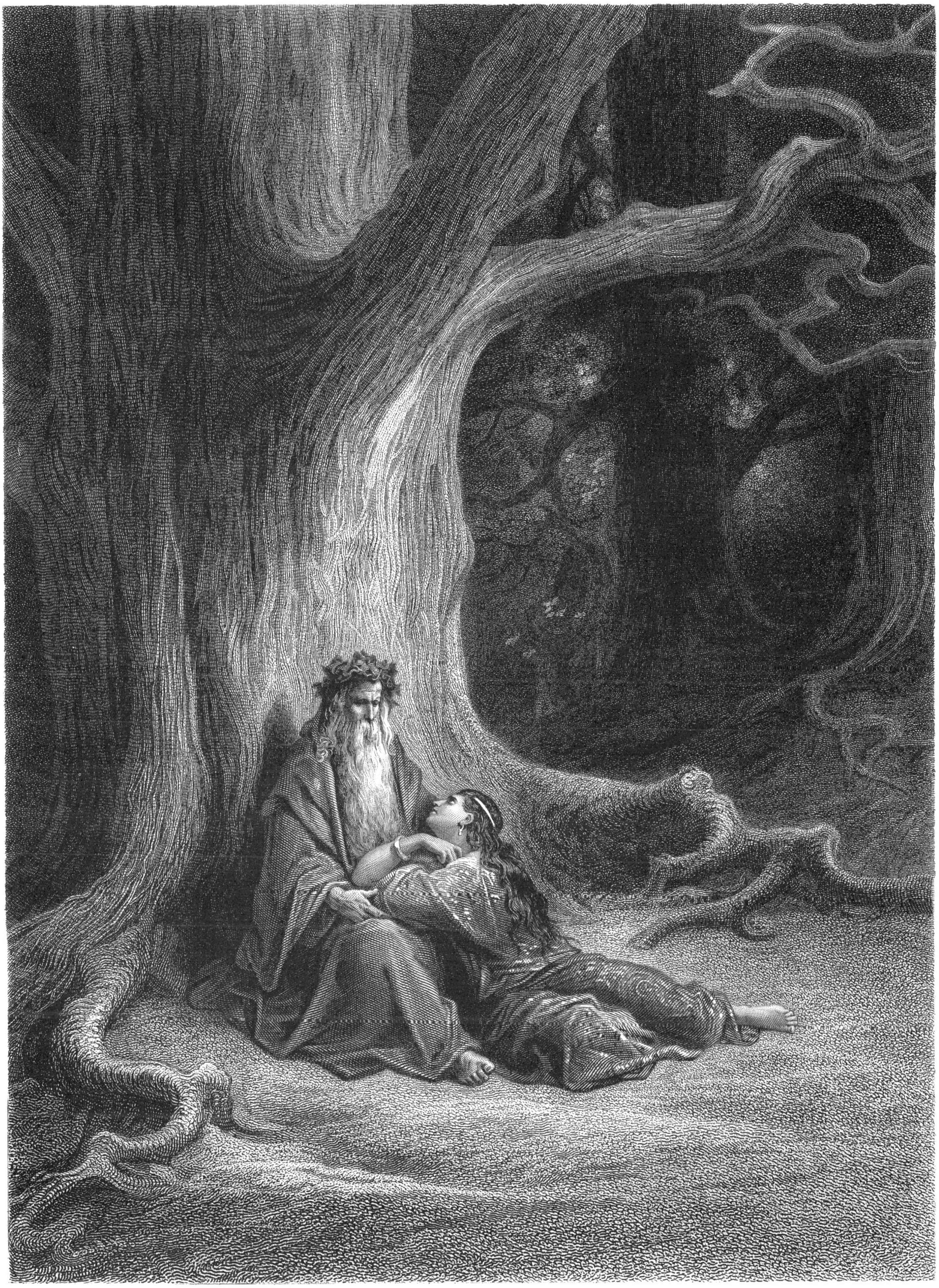

## Plate XI

Vivien, earlier slighted by King Arthur when she tried to seduce him, had become an object of ridicule in Camelot. She plans her revenge by setting out "to gain / Him, the most famous man of all those times, / Merlin." To this end, she pursues the wizard, pretending to be in love: "She played about with slight and sprightly talk, / And vivid smiles . . . / . . . would often when they met / Sigh fully, or all-silent gaze upon him / With such a fixt devotion, that the old man, / Tho' doubtful, felt the flattery." Merlin "half-believes" Vivien loves him, but wavers even while she remains "fixt in her will" to seduce him.

> Then fell upon him a great melancholy;
> And leaving Arthur's court he gain'd the beach;
> There found a little boat, and stept into it;
> And Vivien follow'd, but he mark'd her not.
> She took the helm and he the sail; the boat
> Drave with a sudden wind across the deeps,
> And touching Breton sands, they disembark'd. (45–51)

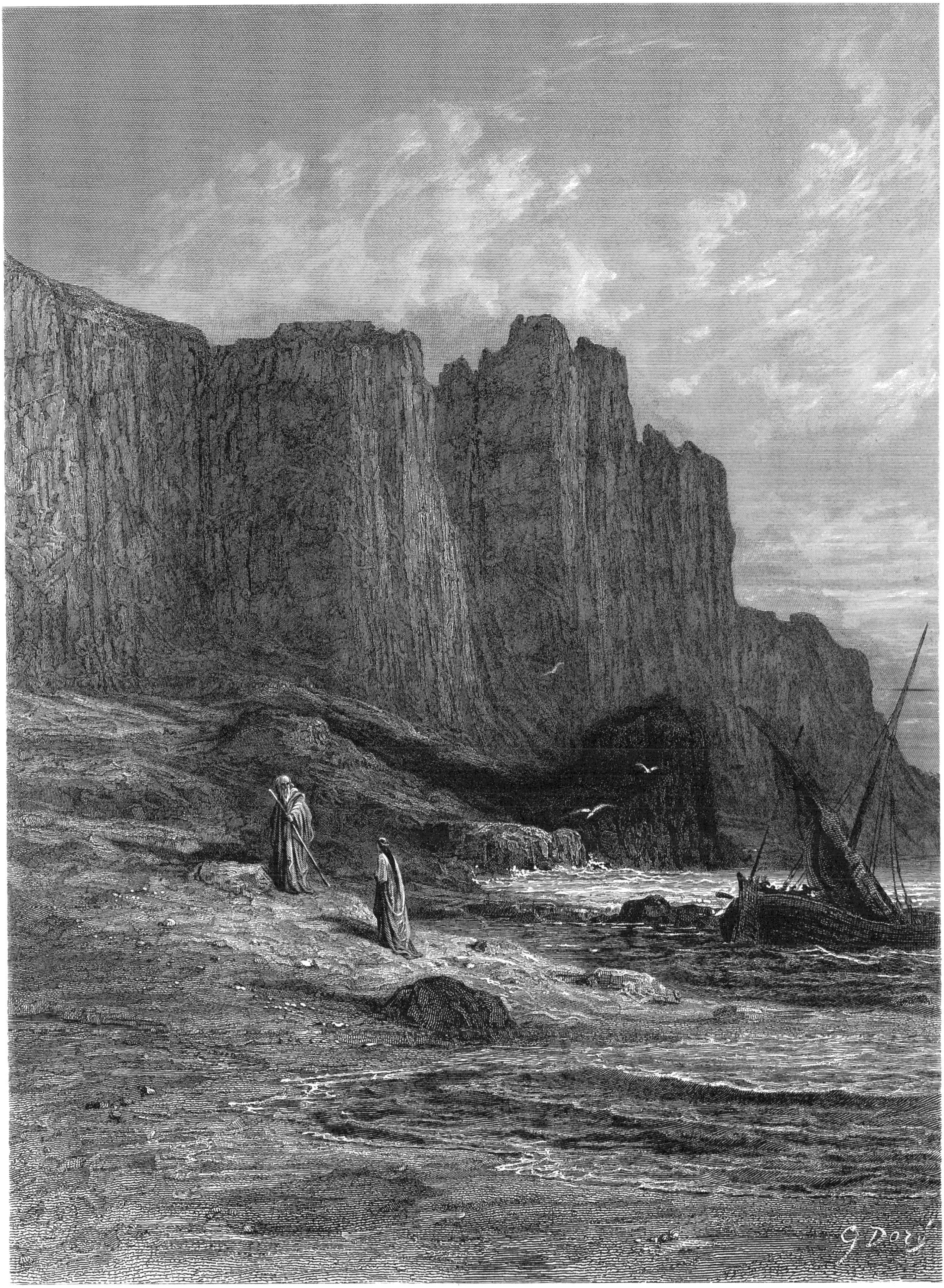
G. Doré

# Plate XII

Having sailed across the channel to Brittany, Merlin proceeds toward the legendary woods of Broceliande. Merlin continues to ignore Vivien, and she to follow him.

And then she follow'd Merlin all the way,
Ev'n to the wild woods of Broceliande.
For Merlin once had told her of a charm,
The which if any wrought on any one
With woven paces and with waving arms,
The man so wrought on ever seem'd to lie
Closed in the four walls of a hollow tower,
From which was no escape for evermore;
. . . and he lay as dead
And lost to life and use and name and fame.
And Vivien ever sought to work the charm
Upon the great Enchanter of the Time,
As fancying that her glory would be great
According to his greatness whom she quench'd. (52–67)

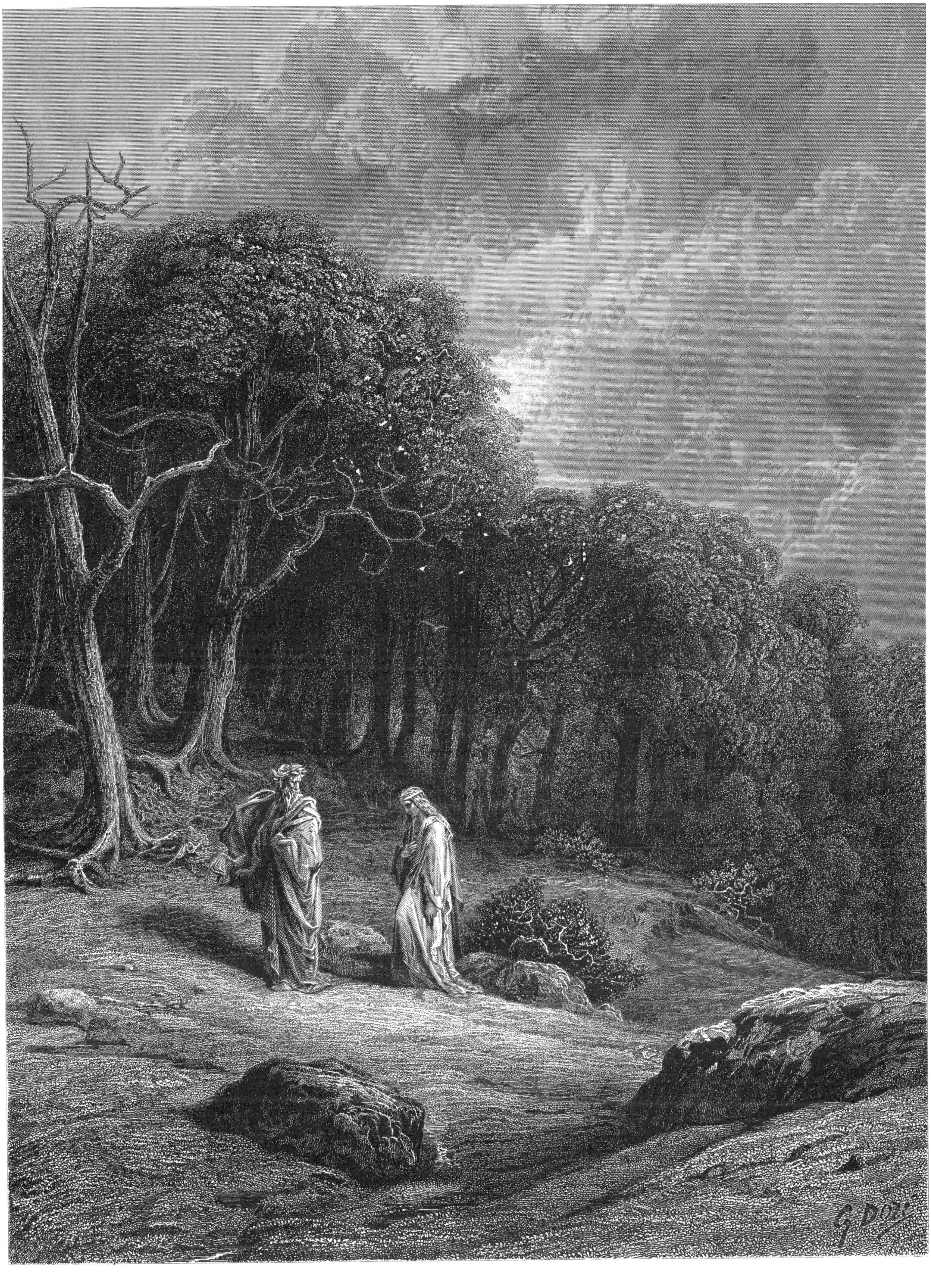
G. Doré

# Plate XIII

As the two sit underneath the tree, Merlin remains silent. In response to her repeated question, "O Merlin, do you love me?" Merlin finally asks, "To what request for what strange boon . . . / Are these your pretty tricks and fooleries, / O Vivien, the preamble?" Vivien acts offended, particularly by Merlin's confession that his melancholy is caused by a dark foreboding that she, Vivien, will "sweep me from my hold upon the world, / My use and name and fame." Half-convinced by Vivien's protestations, Merlin asks her pardon. Vivien then requests that Merlin teach her the magic charm to prove that he trusts her. When he refuses, she sings a song about the necessity for complete trust between lovers, and "So tender was her voice, so fair her face, / So sweetly gleam'd her eyes behind her tears" that Merlin is almost convinced of her sincerity. Nevertheless, thoughts of his past with King Arthur intrude, and Merlin combats Vivien's attraction with his memories.

"Far other was the song that once I heard
By this huge oak, sung nearly where we sit:
For here we met, some ten or twelve of us,
To chase a creature that was current then
In these wild woods, the hart with golden horns.
It was the time when first the question rose
About the founding of a Table Round,
That was to be, for love of God and men
And noble deeds, the flower of all the world.
And each incited each to noble deeds." (255–264)

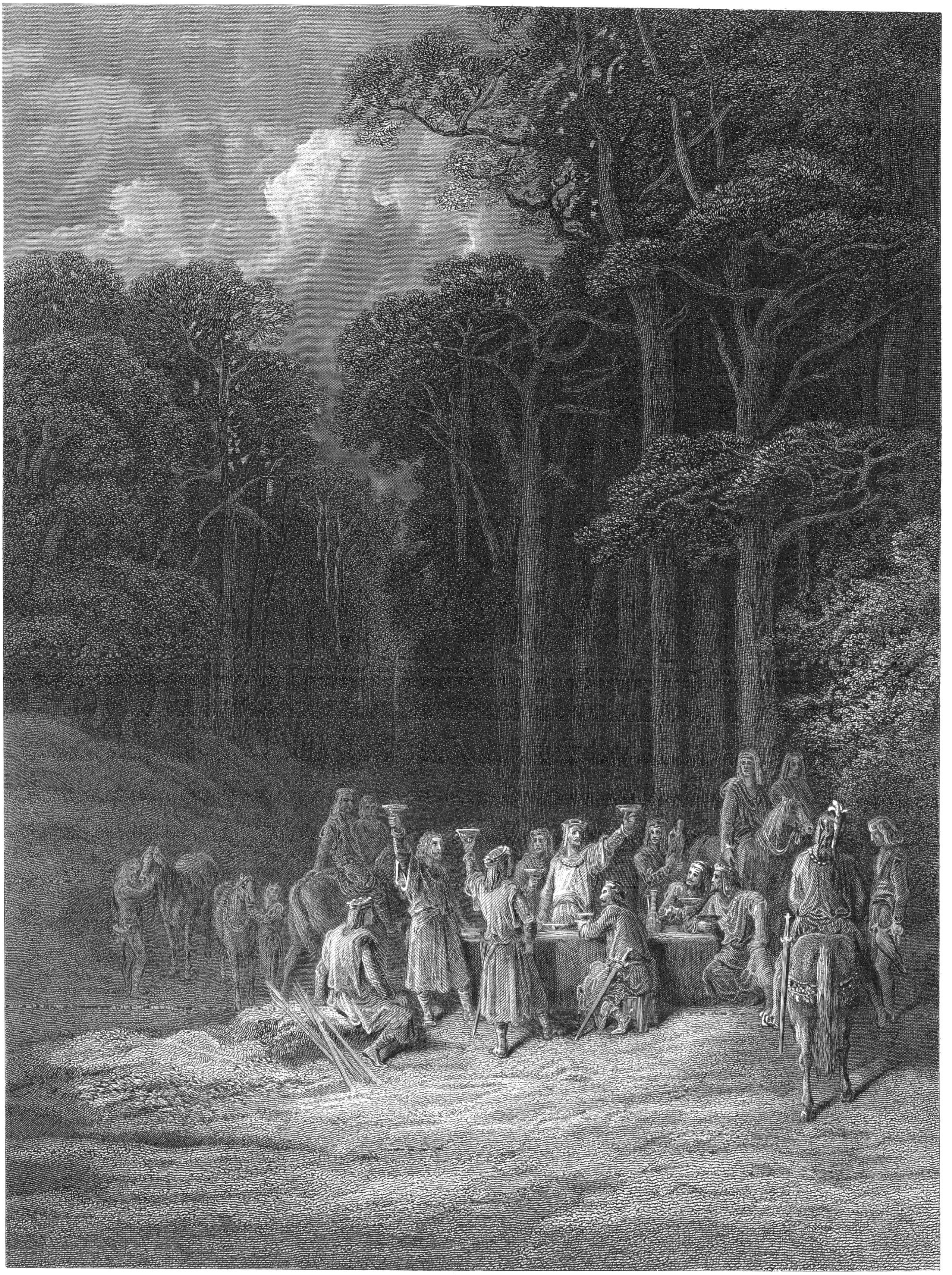

# Plate XIV

Merlin continues his reminiscences of the Round Table's beginnings. The youngest of the knights became so enthusiastic at the talk of chivalry that he "flash'd" into song. His enthusiasm was contagious and the others joined in—startling their prey, the hart with the golden horns. It

"like a silver shadow slipt away
Thro' the dim land; and all day long we rode
Thro' the dim land against a rushing wind,
That glorious roundel echoing in our ears,
And chased the flashes of his golden horns
Until they vanished by the fairy well
That laughs at iron—as our warriors did—
Where children cast their pins and nails, and cry,
'Laugh, little well,' but touch it with a sword,
It buzzes wildly round the point; and there
We lost him: such a noble song was that.
But, Vivien, when you sang me that sweet rhyme,
I felt as tho' you knew this cursed charm,
Were proving it on me, and that I lay
And felt them slowly ebbing, name and fame." (274–288)

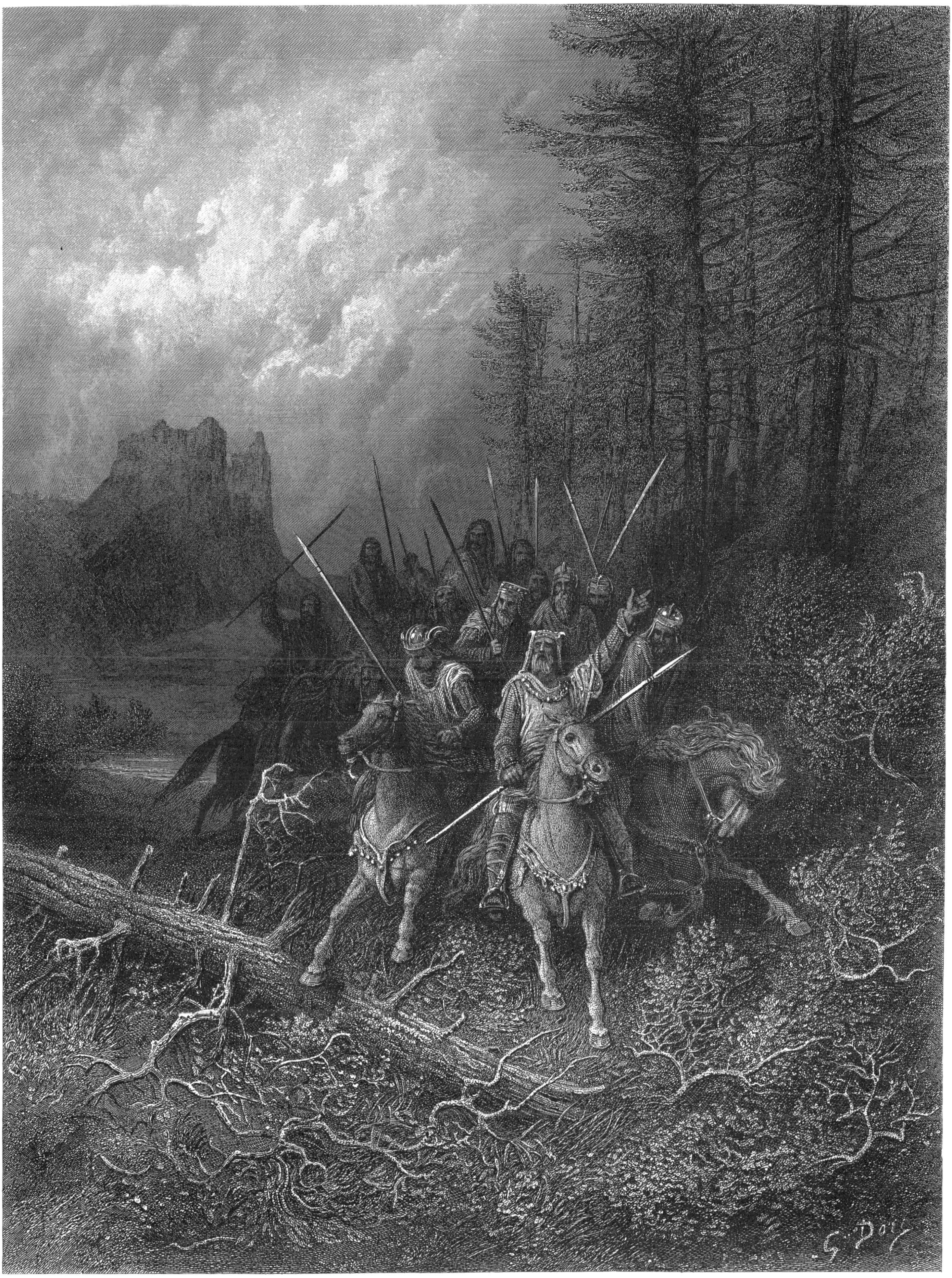

# Plate XV

A DISCUSSION ARISES between Merlin and Vivien about fame. Vivien claims she has given up both name and fame by following Merlin in order to comfort him. But this, she continues, is a typical sacrifice women make for the men they love, for "Man dreams of Fame while woman wakes to love." Merlin then relates an incident to illustrate his feelings about fame:

> "I once was looking for a magic weed,
> And found a fair young squire who sat alone,
> Had carved himself a knightly shield of wood,
> And then was painting on it fancied arms,
> Azure, an Eagle rising or, the Sun
> In dexter chief; the scroll 'I follow fame.'
> And speaking not, but leaning over him,
> I took his brush and blotted out the bird,
> And made a Gardener putting in a graff,
> With this for motto, 'Rather use than fame.'
> You should have seen him blush; but afterwards
> He made a stalwart knight." (322–333)

Even though Merlin's fame has made him vulnerable to the envy and malice of others, it is nevertheless the "ampler means to serve mankind." Merlin desires only to be useful to Arthur, and despite the drawbacks of fame, he must concede that it enables him to be more useful. If Merlin were to agree to Vivien's request and give her the secret charm, he argues, she might use it against him—and he would lose the ability to serve the King.

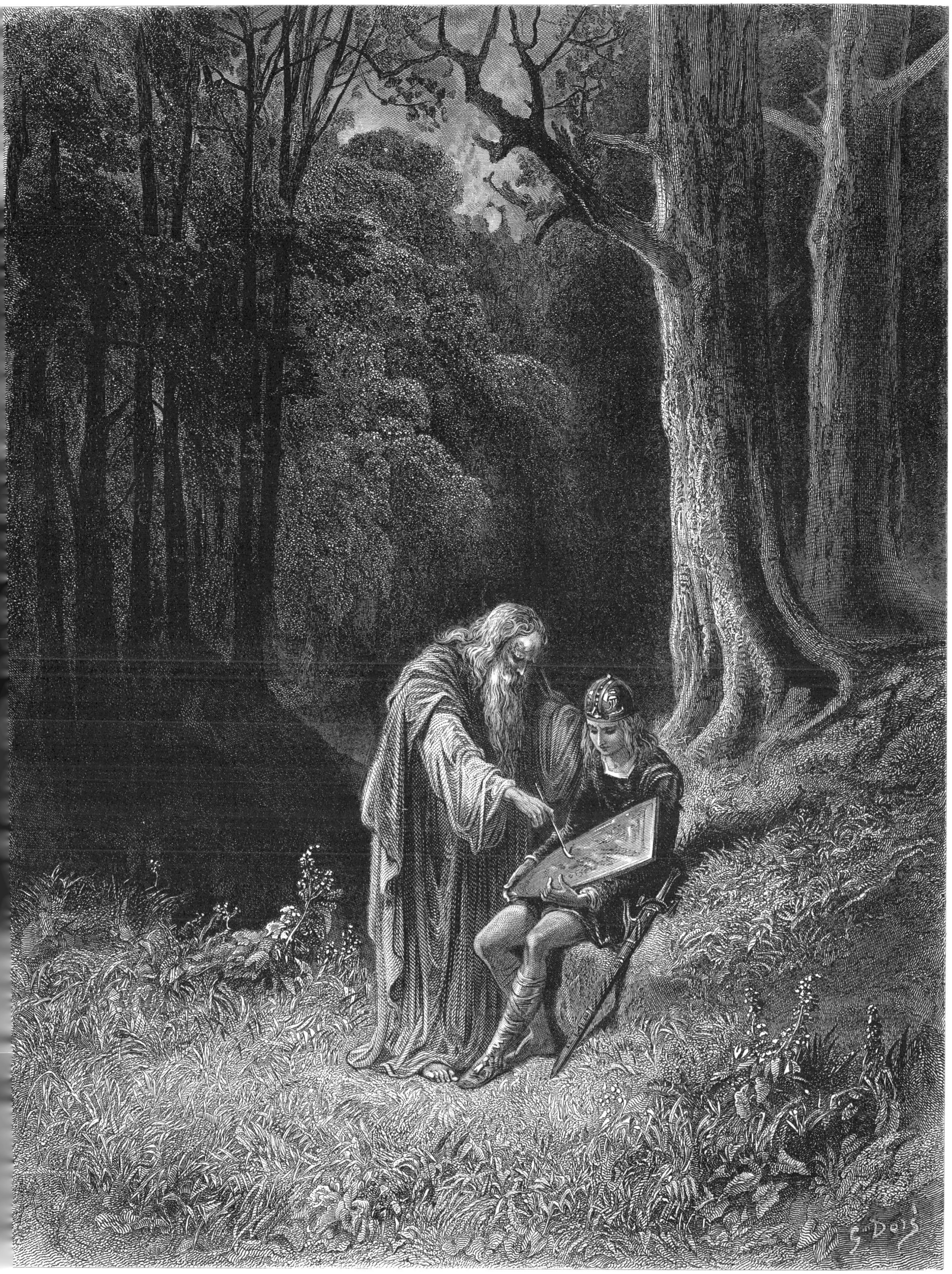

# Plate XVI

Vivien responds to Merlin's refusal by teasing him, telling him that he has probably used the charm to "cage a buxom captive here and there, / Closed in the four walls of a hollow tower / From which is no escape for evermore." Merlin, amused by her raillery, answers in kind, and in lieu of the charm itself, tells her its history.

"There lived a king in the most Eastern East. . . .
A tawny pirate anchor'd in his port,
Whose bark had plunder'd twenty nameless isles;
And passing one, at the high peep of dawn,
He saw two cities in a thousand boats
All fighting for a woman on the sea.
And pushing his black craft among them all,
He lightly scatter'd theirs and brought her off,
With loss of half his people arrow-slain;
A maid so smooth, so white, so wonderful,
They said a light came from her when she moved:
And since the pirate would not yield her up,
The King impaled him for his piracy;
Then made her Queen: but those isle-nurtur'd eyes
Waged such unwilling tho' successful war
On all the youth, they sicken'd; councils thinn'd,
And armies waned, for magnet-like she drew
The rustiest iron of old fighters' hearts;
And beasts themselves would worship. . . .
What wonder, being jealous, that he sent
His horns of proclamation out thro' all
The hundred under-kingdoms that he sway'd
To find a wizard who might teach the King
Some charm, which being wrought upon the Queen
Might keep her all his own." (406–436)

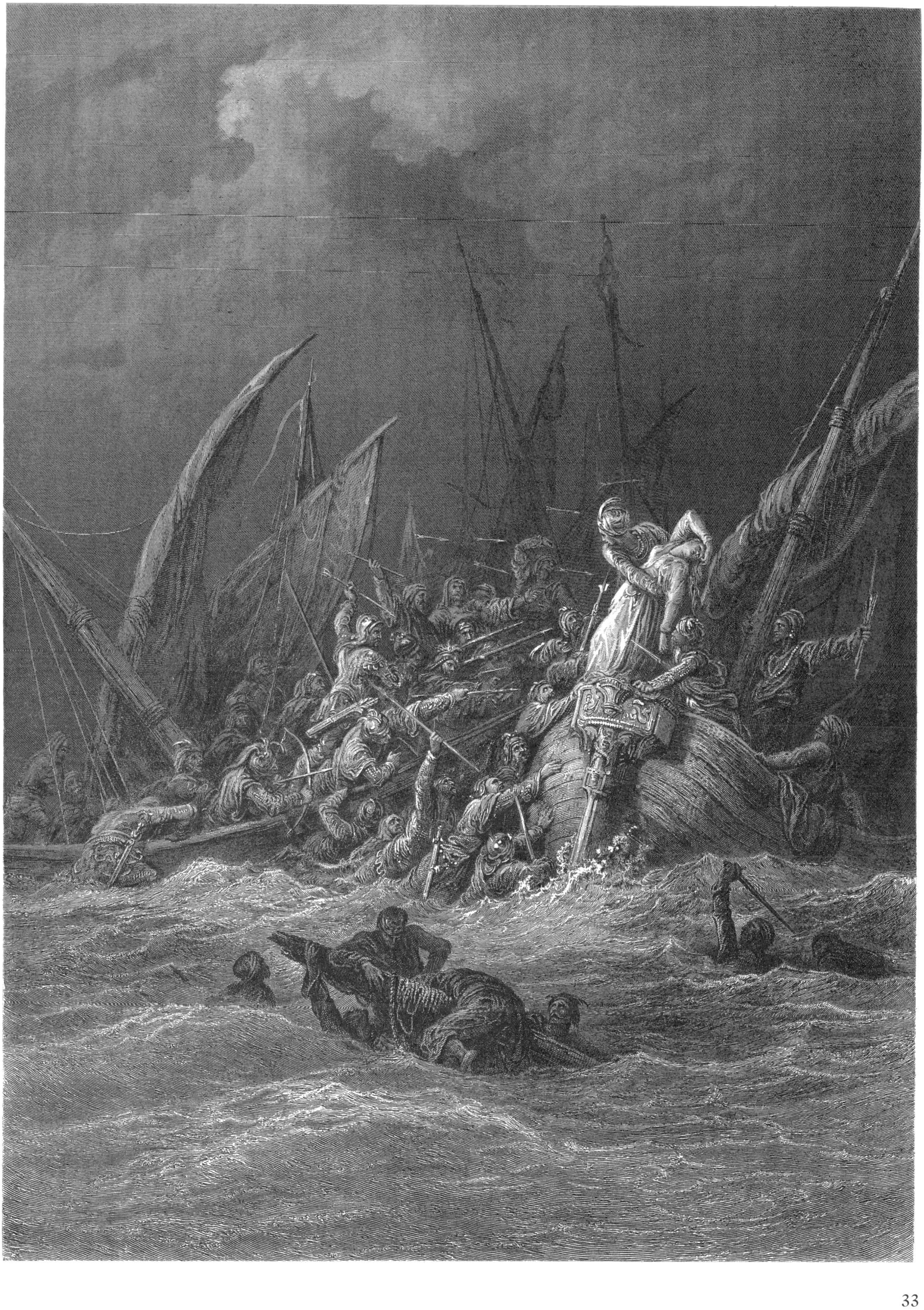

# Plate XVII

Vivien interrupts Merlin's story at this point to tease and criticize him. The Queen, she is certain, had pleasure in the effect she had on men, and most likely gave the king good cause for his jealousy. And, Vivien continues, even if the Queen were as "tame" as Merlin says, there would have been plenty of forsaken and jealous lovers to put an end to her conquests. Despite these faults in his tale, Vivien desires to hear the rest and Merlin continues.

"At last they found—his foragers for charms—
A little glassy-headed hairless man,
Who lived alone in a great wild on grass;
Read but one book, and ever reading grew
So grated down and filed away with thought,
So lean his eyes were monstrous; while the skin
Clung but to crate and basket, ribs and spine.
And since he kept his mind on one sole aim,
Nor touch'd fierce wine, nor tasted flesh,
Nor own'd a sensual wish, to him the wall
That sunders ghosts and shadow-casting men
Became a crystal, and he saw them thro' it,
And heard their voices talk behind the wall,
And learn't their elemental secrets, powers
And forces. . . .
And so by force they dragged him to the King.
And then he taught the King to charm the Queen
In such-wise, that no man could see her more,
Nor saw she save the King, who wrought the charm,
Coming and going, and she lay as dead,
And lost all use of life." (470–496)

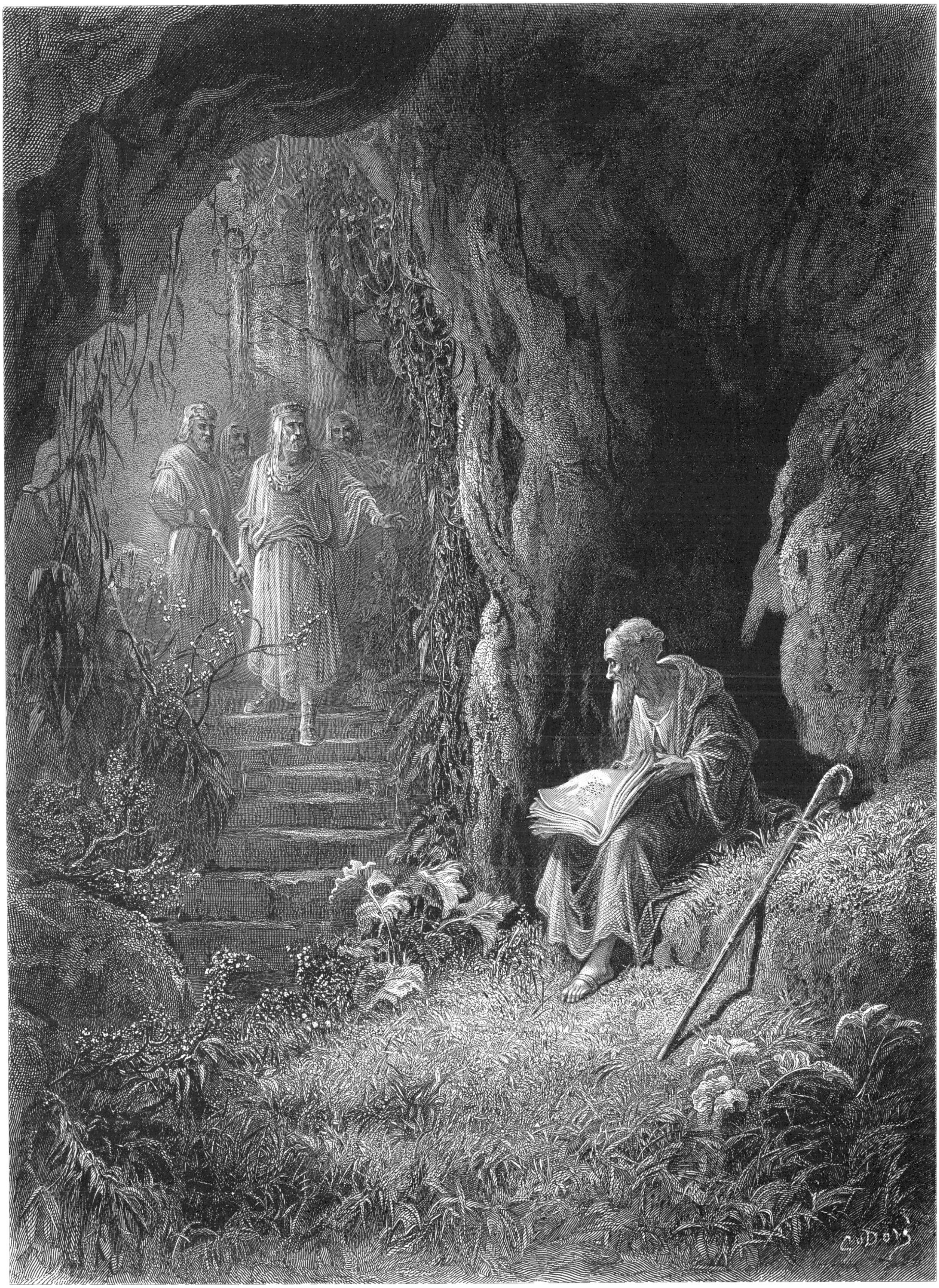

# Plate XVIII

Merlin once again refuses to give Vivien the charm—for he realizes that though she might not use it on him, she might bewitch one of the knights of the Round Table, "And all because you dream they babble of you." This, of course, is Vivien's reason for plotting against the wizard, and for the first time she responds to Merlin's words in "true anger." At Merlin's prompting she brings specific charges against many of the knights, each of whom Merlin defends. But when Vivien speaks spitefully of Arthur, "blameless King and stainless man," Merlin is convinced of her treachery. Vivien realizes that Merlin has seen through her flattery, but nevertheless she keeps up the pretense of wounded lover. As she turns to leave him—acting the part of "A virtuous gentlewoman deeply wrong'd"—the approaching storm breaks. Against the dark background Merlin weakens, and as he protects Vivien from the fury of the storm, he "half believed her true." Vivien takes advantage of Merlin's weakness, and exacts her revenge.

> [T]he storm, its burst of passion spent,
> Moaning and calling out of other lands,
> Had left the ravaged woodland yet once more
> To peace; and what should not have been had been,
> For Merlin, overtalk'd and overworn,
> Had yielded, told her all the charm, and slept.
> Then, in one moment, she put forth the charm
> Of woven paces and of waving hands,
> And in the hollow oak he lay as dead,
> And lost to life and use and name and fame.
> Then crying "I have made his glory mine,"
> And shrieking out "O fool!" the harlot leapt
> Adown the forest, and the thicket closed
> Behind her, and the forest echo'd "fool." (811–824)

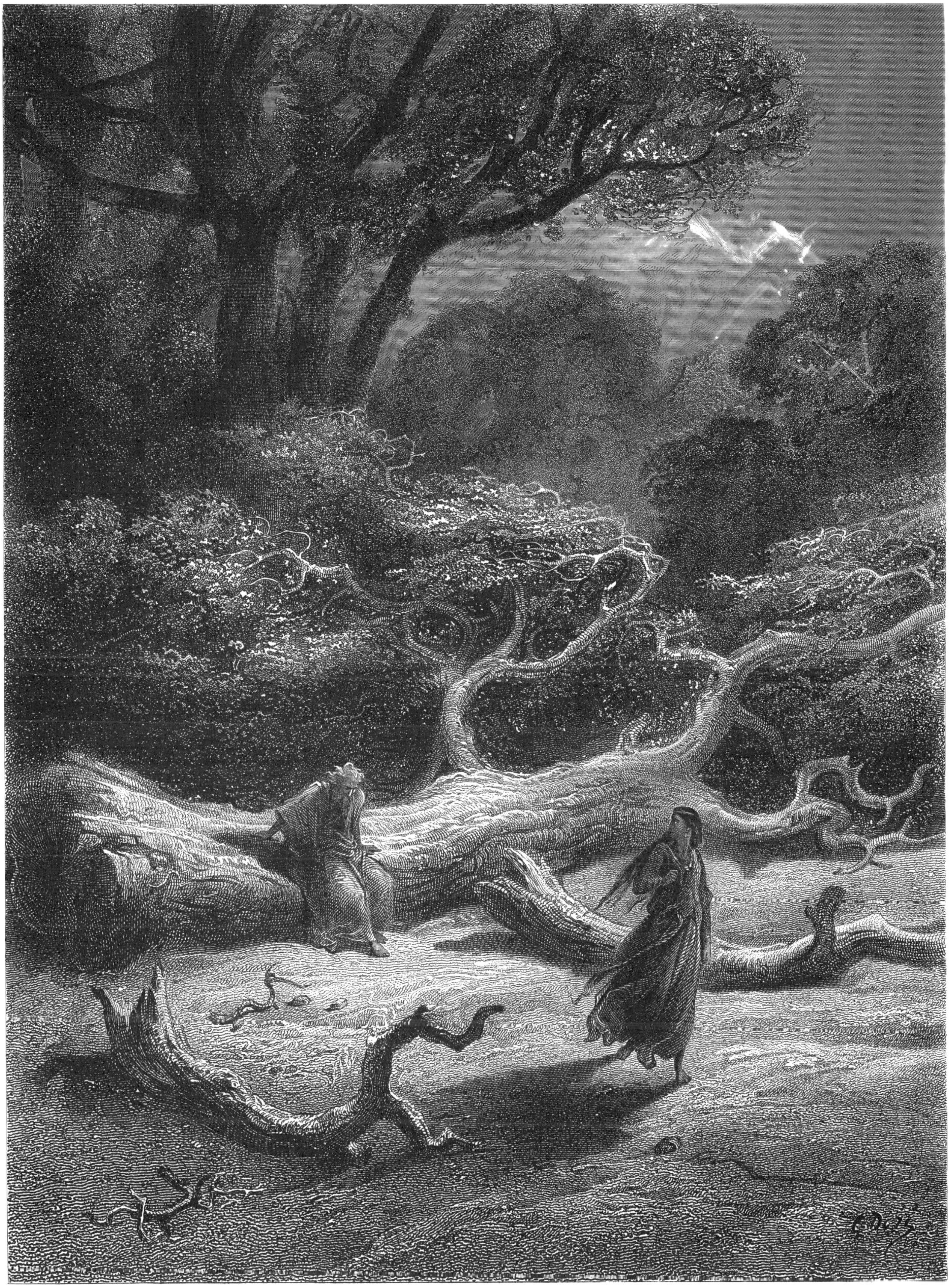

# ELAINE

## PLATE XIX

THE STORY OF Elaine, "the lily maid of Astolat," opens with Elaine guarding the shield of Lancelot, the greatest of Arthur's knights. Lancelot has left the shield with Elaine before going to "tilt / For the great diamond in the diamond joust," an annual contest ordained by King Arthur.

One day, Arthur—before he was king—was out "Roving the trackless realms of Lyonnesse," when he came upon the ancient site of a great battle between two brothers, both of whom were killed. One of the brothers had been a king, and had worn a crown "of diamonds, one in front and four aside."

Arthur came, and labouring up the pass
All in a misty moonshine, unawares
Had trodden that crown'd skeleton, and the skull
Brake from the nape, and from the skull the crown
Roll'd into light, and turning on its rim
Fled like a glittering rivulet to the tarn:
And down the shingly scaur he plunged, and caught,
And set it on his head, and in his heart
Heard murmurs "lo, thou likewise shalt be king." (48–56)

Once Arthur became king, he had the nine diamonds taken out of the crown and declared that each year, one stone would be given to the winner of the joust.

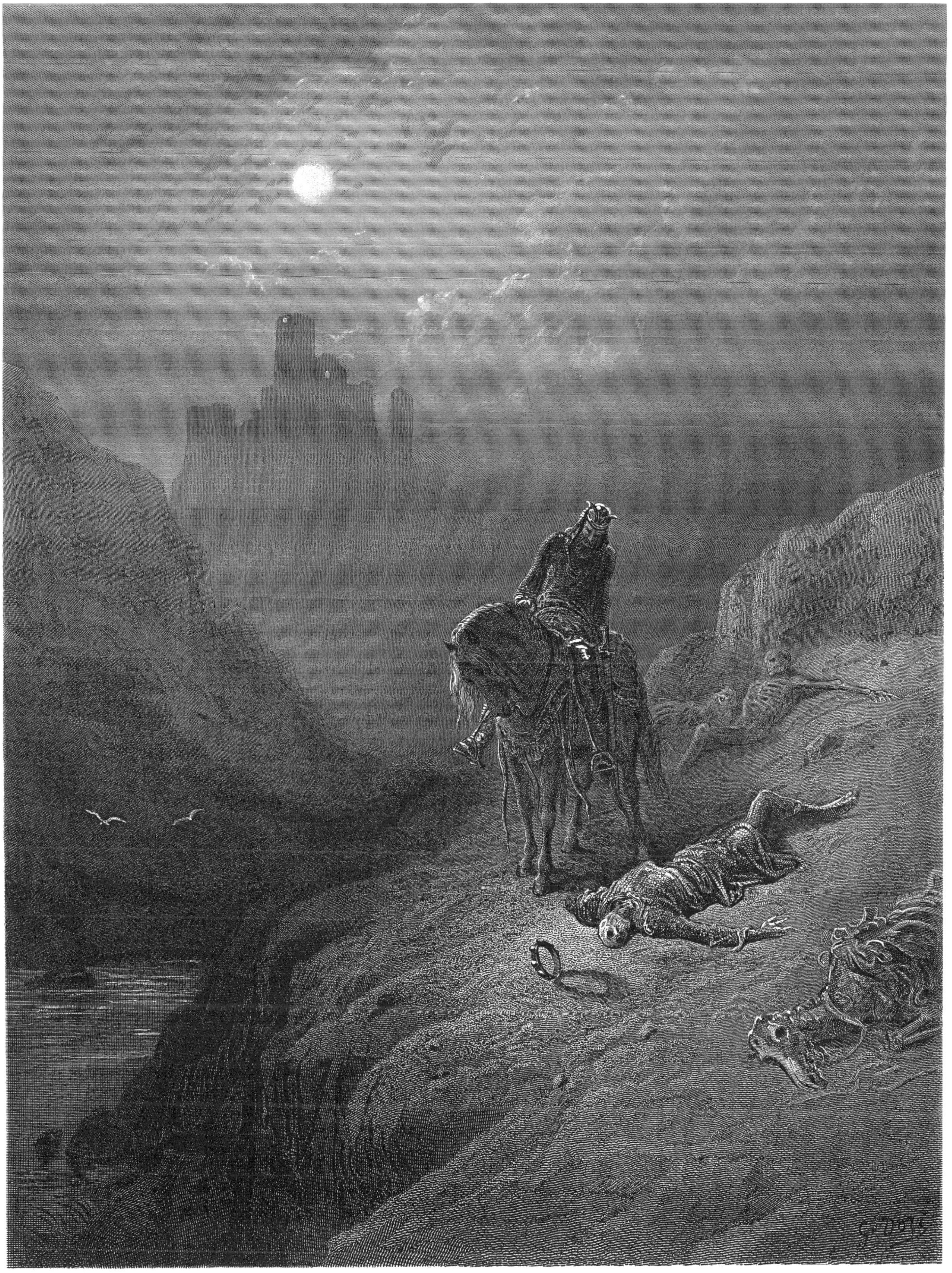

# Plate XX

For the past eight years, Lancelot has won each of the diamonds at the tournament. On this, the last year, he determines to win the ninth so that he can give the entire set to Queen Guinevere. The two have been lovers for many years now, their names linked by court gossip, and their love suspected by everyone but Arthur. As the final diamond joust approaches, Guinevere, who is ill, tells Arthur she cannot go to the tournament. Lancelot, who is present when she says this, mistakenly believes Guinevere wants him to stay with her rather than go to the contest. He lies to Arthur, telling him that an unhealed wound prevents him from participating in the joust. When the two are alone, Guinevere chides Lancelot for lying; they argue, and at last Guinevere suggests that Lancelot go to the joust in disguise. After winning, he can tell Arthur that he participated anonymously so that he, rather than his reputation, could prevail. Lancelot agrees, and the two part.

Then got Sir Lancelot suddenly to horse,
Wroth at himself: not willing to be known,
He left the barren-beaten thoroughfare,
Chose the green path that show'd the rarer foot,
And here among the solitary downs,
Full often lost in fancy, lost his way;
Till as he traced a faintly-shadow'd track,
That all in loops and links among the dales
Ran to the Castle of Astolat, he saw
Fired from the west, far on a hill, the towers. (160–169)

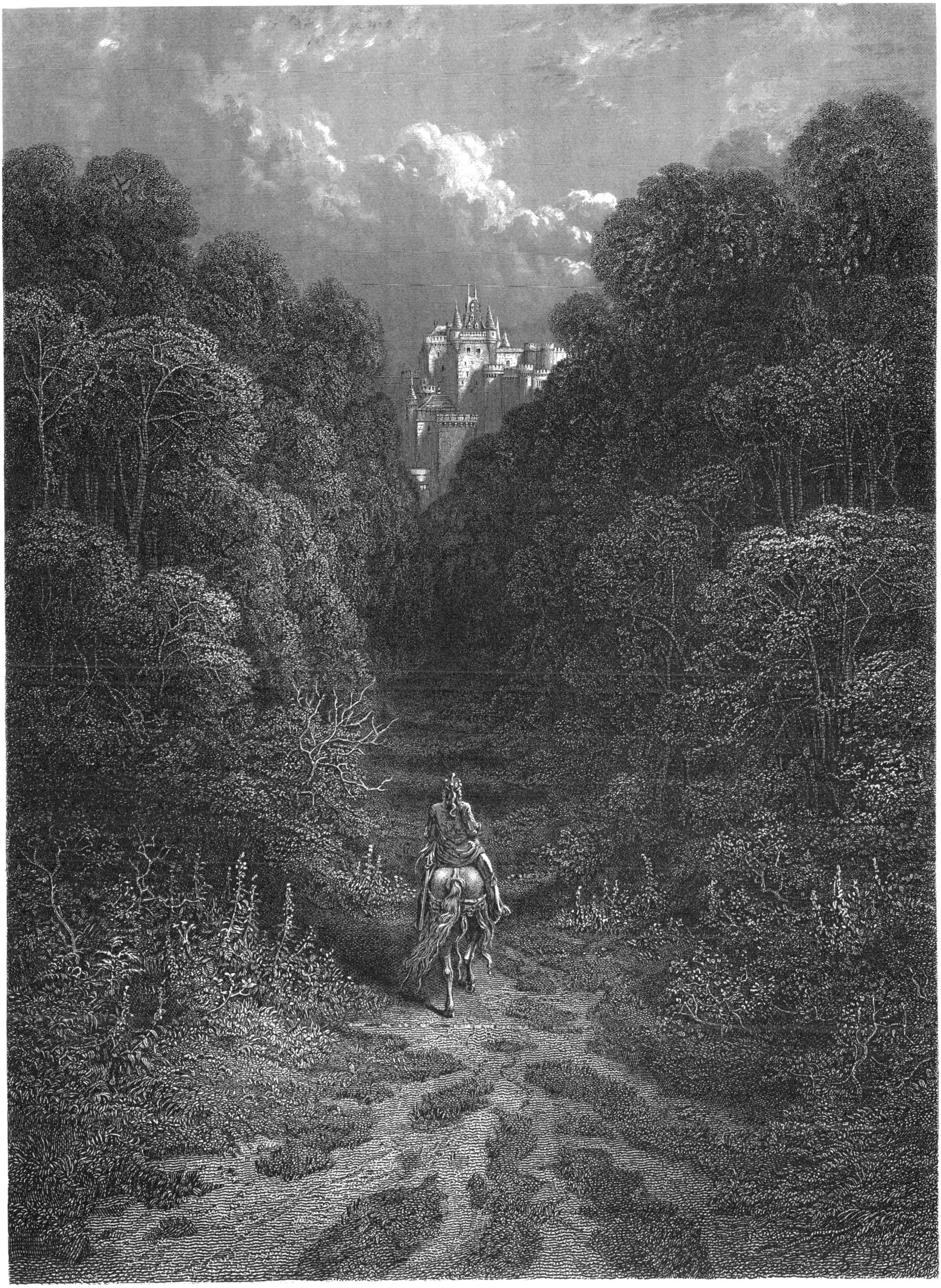

# Plate XXI

At the Castle of Astolat, Lancelot meets the Lord of Astolat, his two sons Sir Torre and Sir Lavaine, and his daughter Elaine. Lancelot explains that he is traveling incognito and is on his way to Camelot to joust for the diamond. But Lancelot has brought with him his own shield, by which he will be recognized unless he can borrow another. It is decided that Lancelot will use Torre's shield, and that Lavaine will accompany him and enter the contest as well—perhaps to win the diamond for Elaine. Lavaine, teasing his sister, reveals that she has had a dream in which "some one put this diamond in her hand, / And that it was too slippery to be held, / And slipt into some pool or stream." As for Elaine, she falls in love with Lancelot immediately, despite his face, which is ravaged by the "great and guilty love he bare the Queen."

Then the great knight, the darling of the court,
Loved of the loveliest, into that rude hall
Stept with all grace, and not with half disdain
Hid under grace, as in smaller time,
But kindly man moving among his kind:
Whom they with meats and vintage of their best
And talk and minstrel melody entertain'd.
And much they ask'd of court and Table Round,
And ever well and readily answer'd he. (262–270)

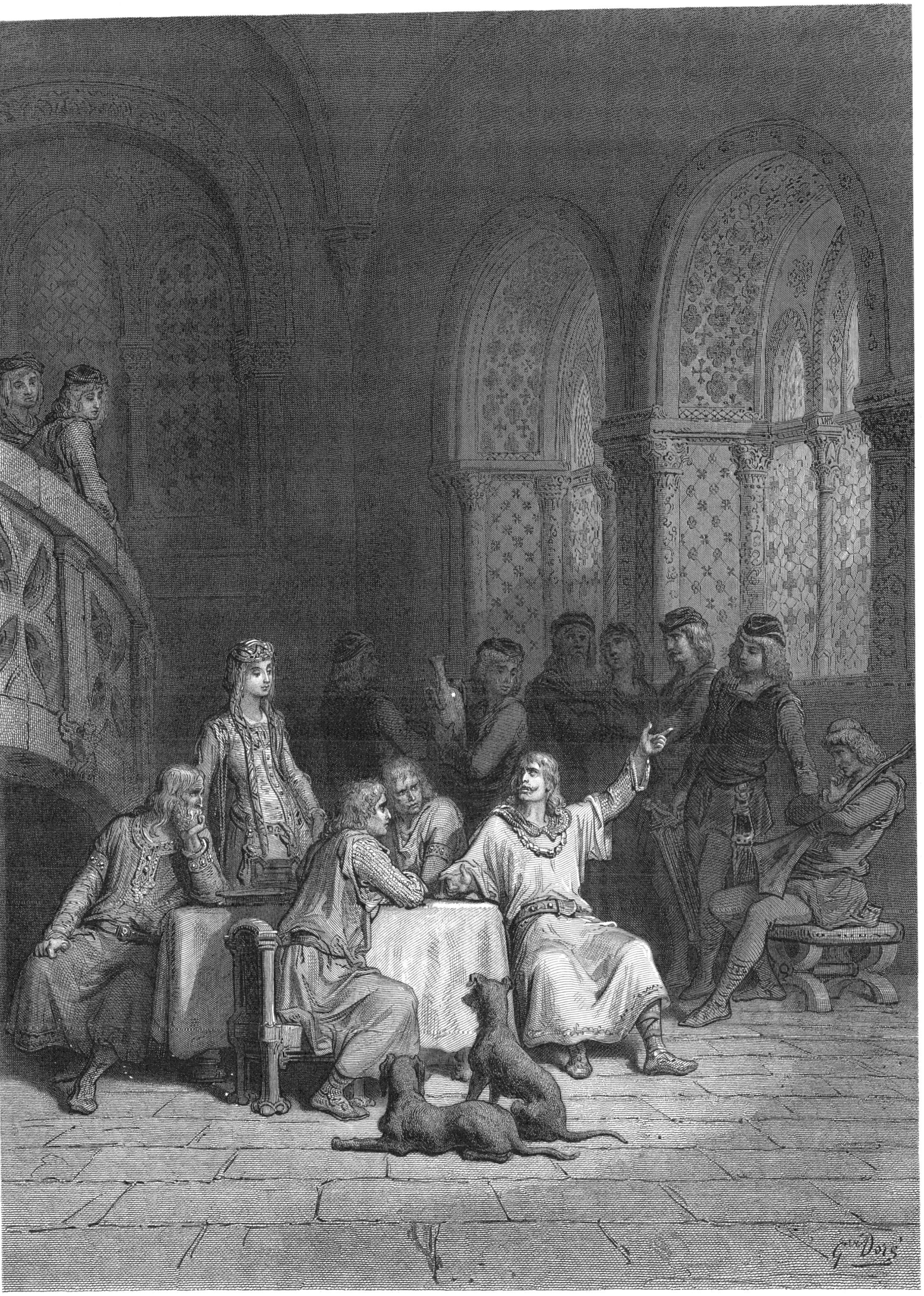

# Plate XXII

Elaine spends the evening thinking of Lancelot, and after a sleepless night, rises to bid farewell to her brother Lavaine. Coming down from her tower she hears Lancelot's voice, and entering the courtyard, she stands watching the knight prepare to depart.

> He look'd, and more amazed
> Than if seven men had set upon him, saw
> The maiden standing in the dewy light.
> He had not dream'd she was so beautiful.
> Then came on him a sort of sacred fear,
> For silent, tho' he greeted her, she stood
> Rapt on his face as if it were a God's.
> Suddenly flash'd on her a wild desire,
> That he should wear her favor at the tilt.
> She braved a riotous heart in asking for it. (351–360)

Lancelot at first refuses Elaine's request on the grounds that he has never worn any woman's favor. But if he wears her favor, Elaine argues, no one who knows him will suspect his identity. Lancelot agrees and asks her to keep his shield until he returns for it. Elaine watches the two knights depart, "Then to her tower she climb'd, and took the shield, / There kept it, and so lived in fantasy."

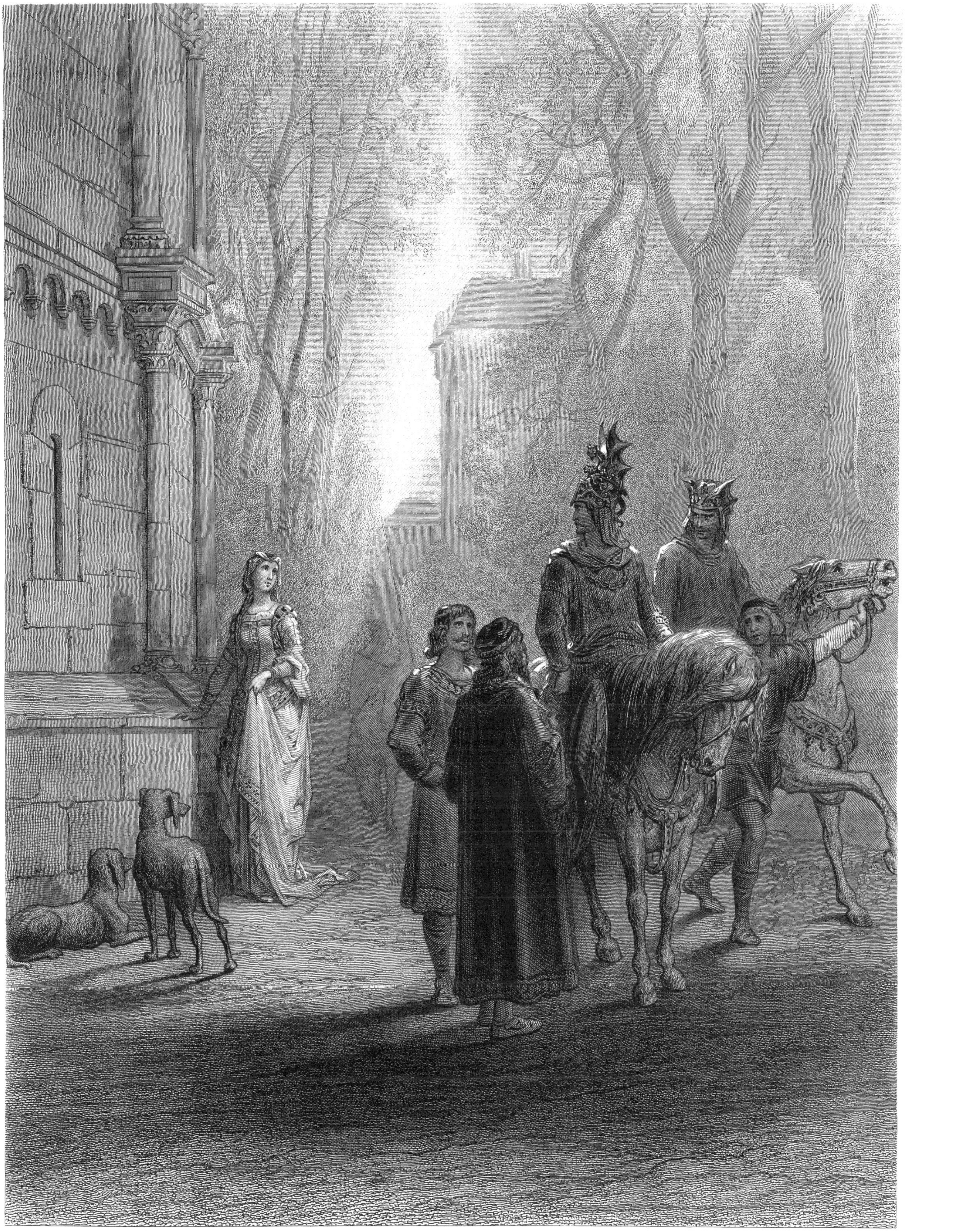

# Plate XXIII

Lancelot, fighting anonymously, wins the tournament, but is severely wounded. He and Lavaine retire to a hermit's cave near Camelot, and there Elaine finds them. She presents Lancelot with the diamond, explaining that Arthur, now aware that Lancelot was the unnamed knight, had charged Sir Gawain to find Lancelot and deliver to him his prize. Gawain, in turn, yielded his quest to Elaine, who has succeeded in finding the knight. Unable to keep her love and concern for Lancelot hidden, "all her heart's sad secret blazed itself / In the heart's colours on her simple face." Lancelot sees this, but since he loves only Guinevere, "he feign'd a sleep until he slept."

Then rose Elaine and glided thro' the fields,
And past beneath the wildly-sculptured gates
Far up the dim rich city to her kin;
There bode the night: but woke with dawn, and past
Down thro' the dim rich city to the fields,
Thence to the cave: so day by day she past
In either twilight ghost-like to and fro
Gliding, and every day she tended him,
And likewise many a night. (853–861)

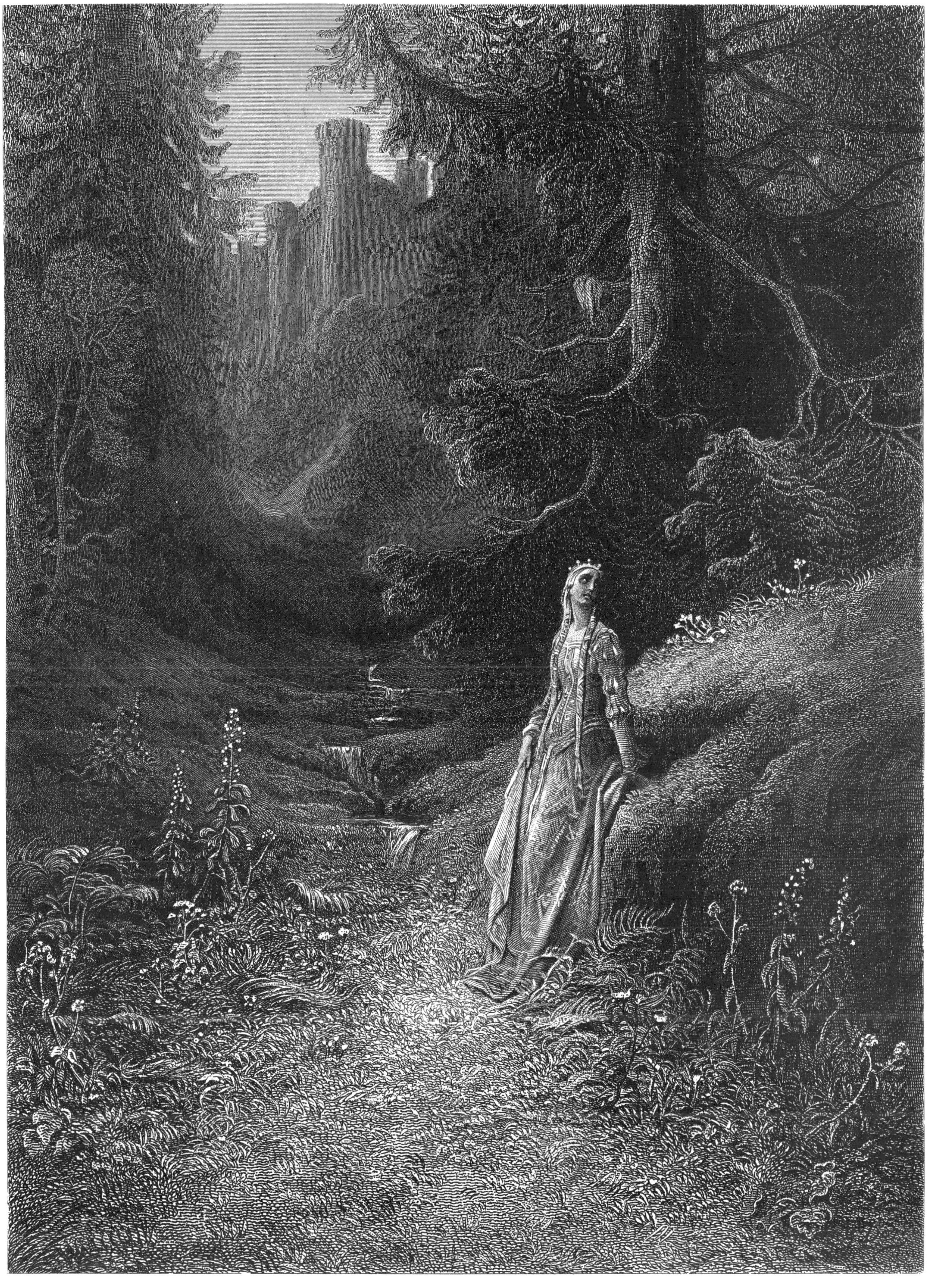

# Plate XXIV

Thanks to Elaine's care, Lancelot eventually recovers from his wound and they return to Astolat. Though Elaine suspects that Lancelot does not return her love, she cherishes her vain hopes. Lancelot, who feels only fraternal love for her, entreats Elaine to accept some gift as a token of his gratitude. Elaine confesses her love for him, and tells him the only thing she wants is to be his wife. Though sympathetic, Lancelot explains that he cannot love her, and he soon departs for Camelot. Resigned at last to the futility of her hopes, Elaine patiently awaits death. She dictates a letter "for Lancelot and the Queen and all the world," and then instructs her father and brothers to carry out her final wishes.

"[W]hen the heat is gone from out my heart,
Then take the little bed on which I died
For Lancelot's love, and deck it like the Queen's
For richness, and me also like the Queen
In all I have of rich, and lay me on it.
And let there be prepared a chariot-bier
To take me to the river, and a barge
Be ready on the river, clothed in black." (1136–1143)

Soon after, Elaine dies, and at dawn the following day, the two brothers accompany the chariot-bier to the river.

So those two brethren from the chariot took
And on the black decks laid her in her bed,
Set in her hand a lily . . .
And kiss'd her quiet brows, and saying to her
"Sister, farewell for ever," and again
"Farewell, sweet sister," parted all in tears. (1166–1172)

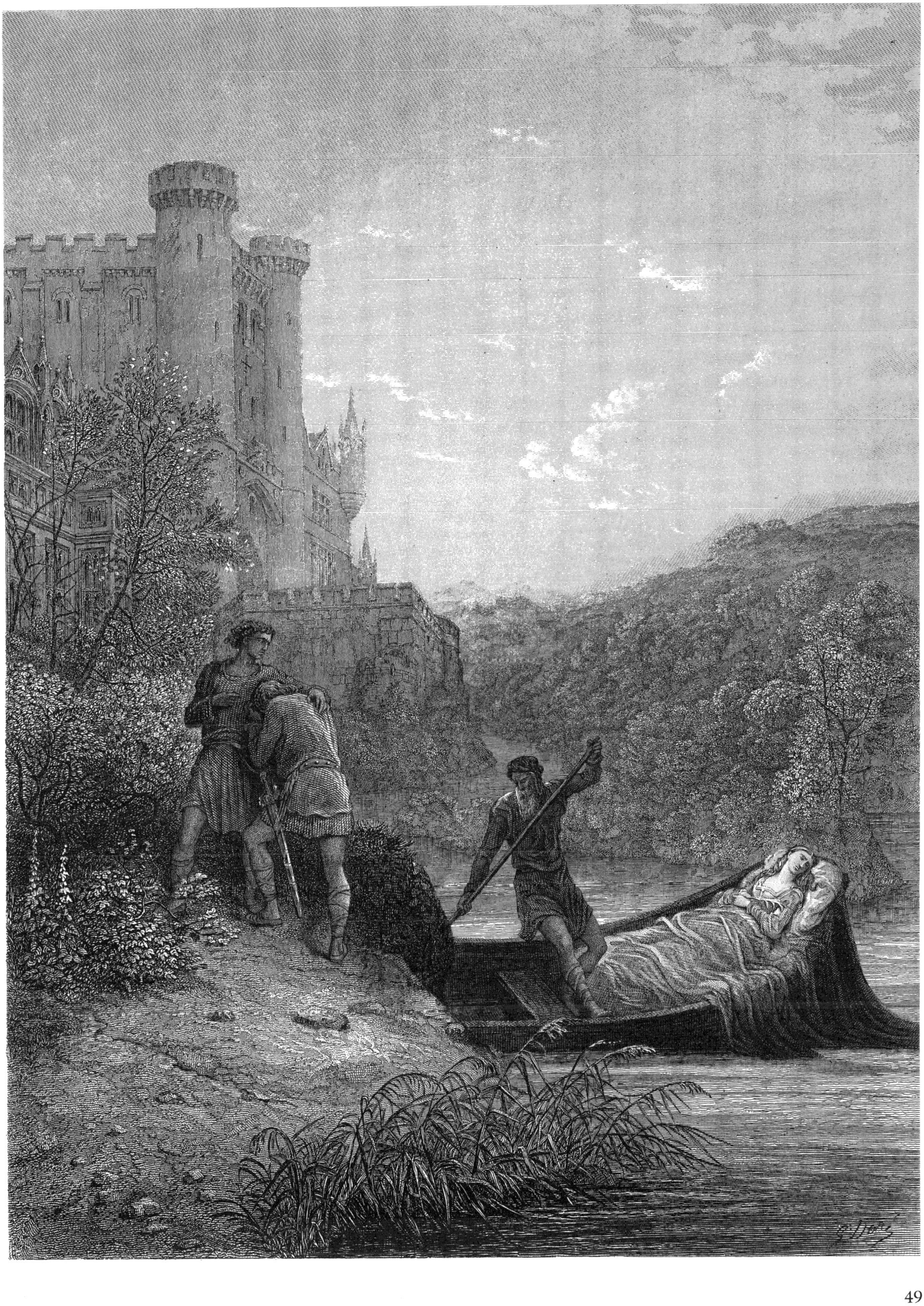

# PLATE XXV

ELAINE'S FUNERAL BARGE is sent down the stream, propelled by a loyal family retainer, an old dumb servant:

> Then rose the dumb old servitor, and the dead
> Steer'd by the dumb went upward with the flood—
> In her right hand the lily, in her left
> The letter—all her bright hair streaming down—
> And all the coverlid was cloth of gold
> Drawn to her waist, and she herself in white
> All but her face, and that clear-featured face
> Was lovely, for she did not seem as dead
> But fast asleep, and lay as tho' she smiled. (1173–1181)

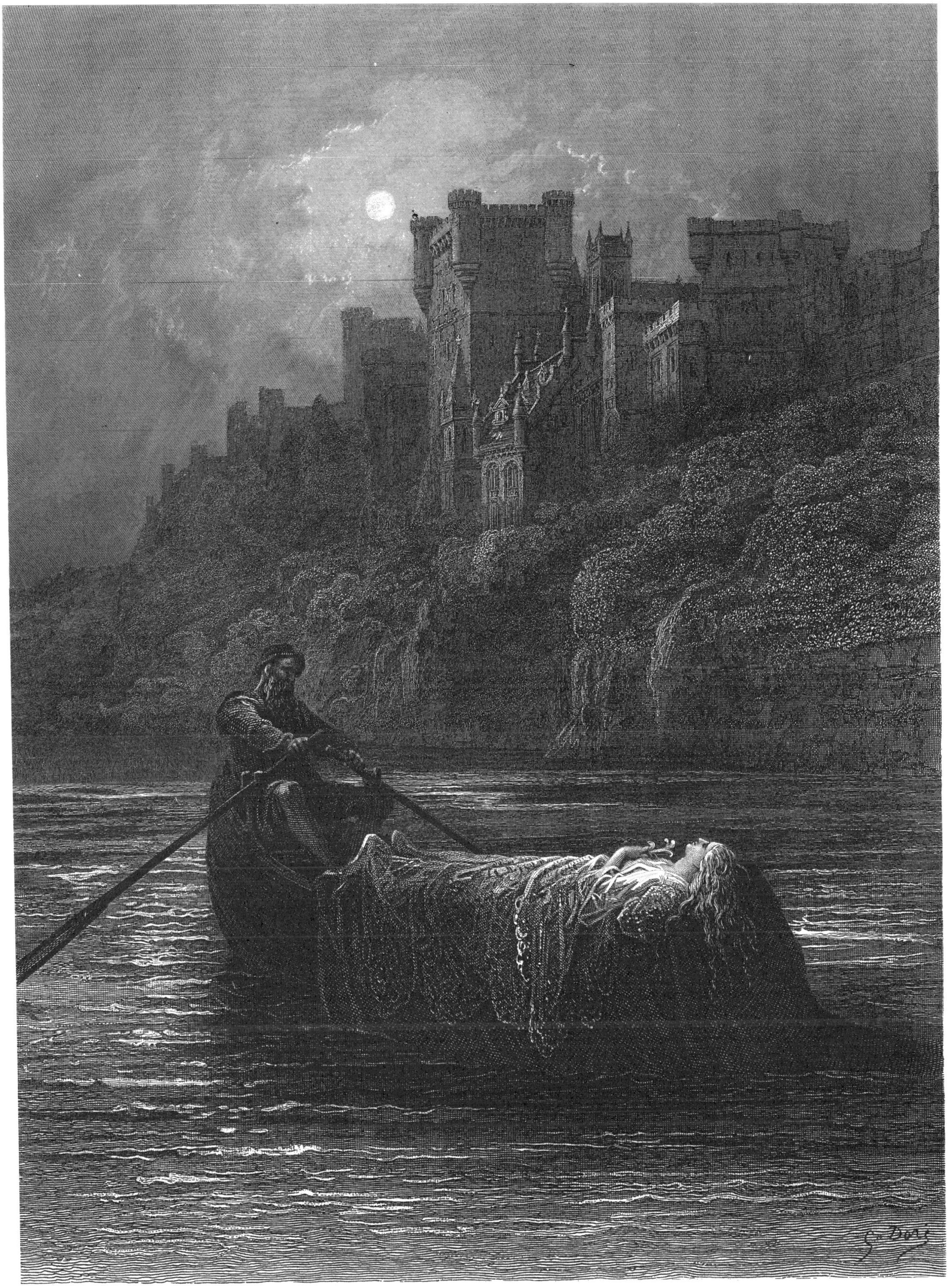
G. Doré

# Plate XXVI

When Elaine's barge arrives at Camelot, she is carried into the hall. There the knights and ladies wonder aloud at her; Lancelot "came and mused at her, / And last the Queen herself and pitied her."

> But Arthur spied the letter in her hand,
> Stoopt, took, brake seal, and read it; this was all.
> "Most noble lord, Sir Lancelot of the Lake,
> I, sometime call'd the maid of Astolat,
> Come, for you left me taking no farewell,
> Hither, to take my last farewell of you.
> I loved you, and my love had no return,
> And therefore my true love has been my death.
> And therefore to our lady Guinevere,
> And to all other ladies, I make moan.
> Pray for my soul, and yield me burial.
> Pray for my soul thou too, Sir Lancelot,
> As thou art a knight peerless."
> Thus he read,
> And ever in the reading, lords and dames
> Wept, looking often from his face who read
> To hers which lay so silent, and at times,
> So touch'd were they, half-thinking that her lips
> Who had devised the letter moved again. (1290–1308)

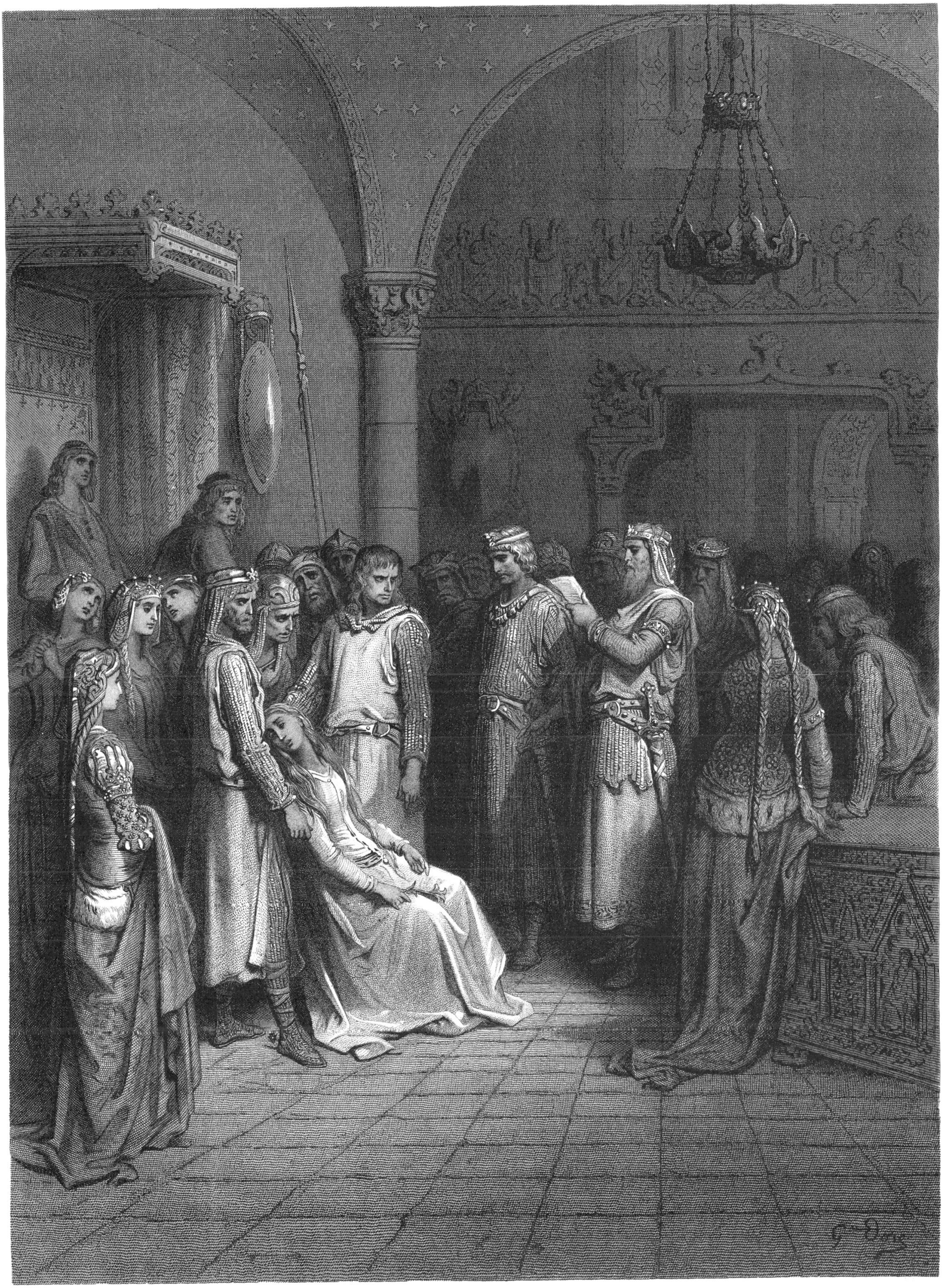

# Plate XXVII

Lancelot, like the rest of the court, is greatly affected by Elaine's letter, though he explains to Arthur that he never encouraged her love. Arthur has her buried "with gorgeous obsequies," and orders an elaborate tomb made, engraved with Elaine's image, with Lancelot's shield at her feet and the lily in her hand; the "story of her dolorous voyage" will also be carved on the tomb for everyone to read. After the funeral, Arthur comes to console Lancelot, who is grieved by Elaine's death. The King expresses mystification at Lancelot's inability to return Elaine's love, but Lancelot, guilty and ashamed, cannot explain that he loves only Guinevere.

And Lancelot answer'd nothing, but he went,
And at the inrunning of a little brook
Sat by the river in a cove, and watch'd
The high reed wave, and lifted up his eyes
And saw the barge that brought her moving down,
Far off, a blot upon the stream, and said
Low in himself . . .
"Alas for Arthur's greatest knight, a man
Not after Arthur's heart! I needs must break
These bonds that so defame me: not without
[Guinevere] wills it: would I, if she will'd it? nay,
Who knows? but if I would not, then may God,
I pray him, send a sudden Angel down
To seize me by the hair and bear me far,
And fling me deep in that forgotten mere,
Among the tumbled fragments of the hills." (1408–1447)

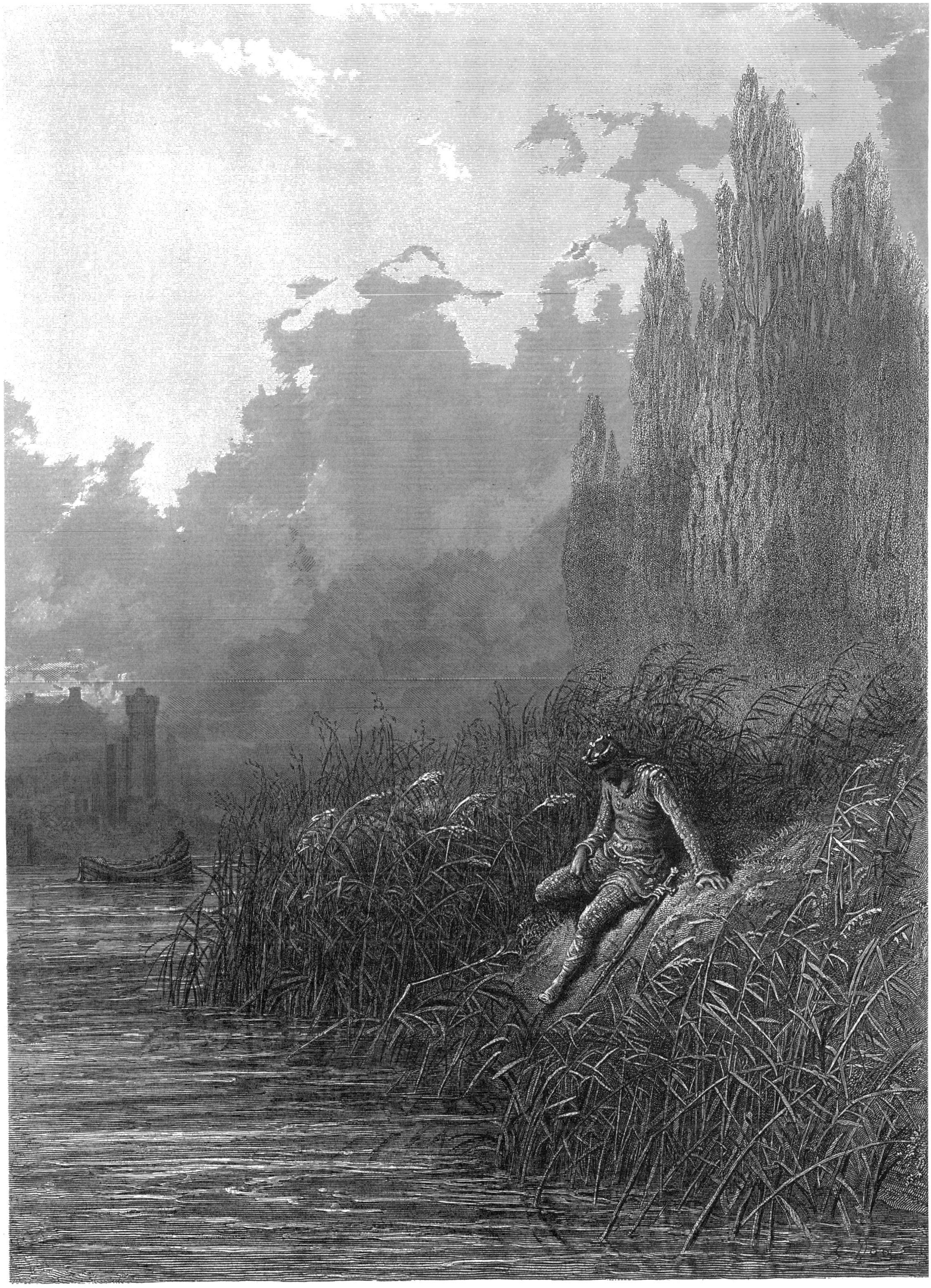

# GUINEVERE

## PLATE XXVIII

THROUGH THE MALICE of Prince Mordred, his nephew, Arthur has learned about Lancelot and Guinevere. Always watchful for an opportunity to cause mischief, Mordred has laid a trap for the lovers, bursting in on them as they meet for one last tryst. Lancelot and the Queen escape, but realize that their secret can now be proved to the King.

[T]hen she [said], "the end is come
And I am shamed for ever;" and he said
"Mine be the shame; mine was the sin: but rise,
And fly to my strong castle overseas:
There will I hide thee, till my life shall end,
There hold thee with my life against the world."
She answer'd "Lancelot, wilt thou hold me so?
Nay friend, for we have taken our farewells.
Would God, that thou couldst hide me from myself!
Mine is the shame, for I was wife, and thou
Unwedded: yet rise now, and let us fly,
For I will draw me into sanctuary,
And bide my doom." So Lancelot got her horse,
Set her thereon, and mounted on his own,
And then they rode to the divided way,
There kiss'd, and parted weeping. (110–125)

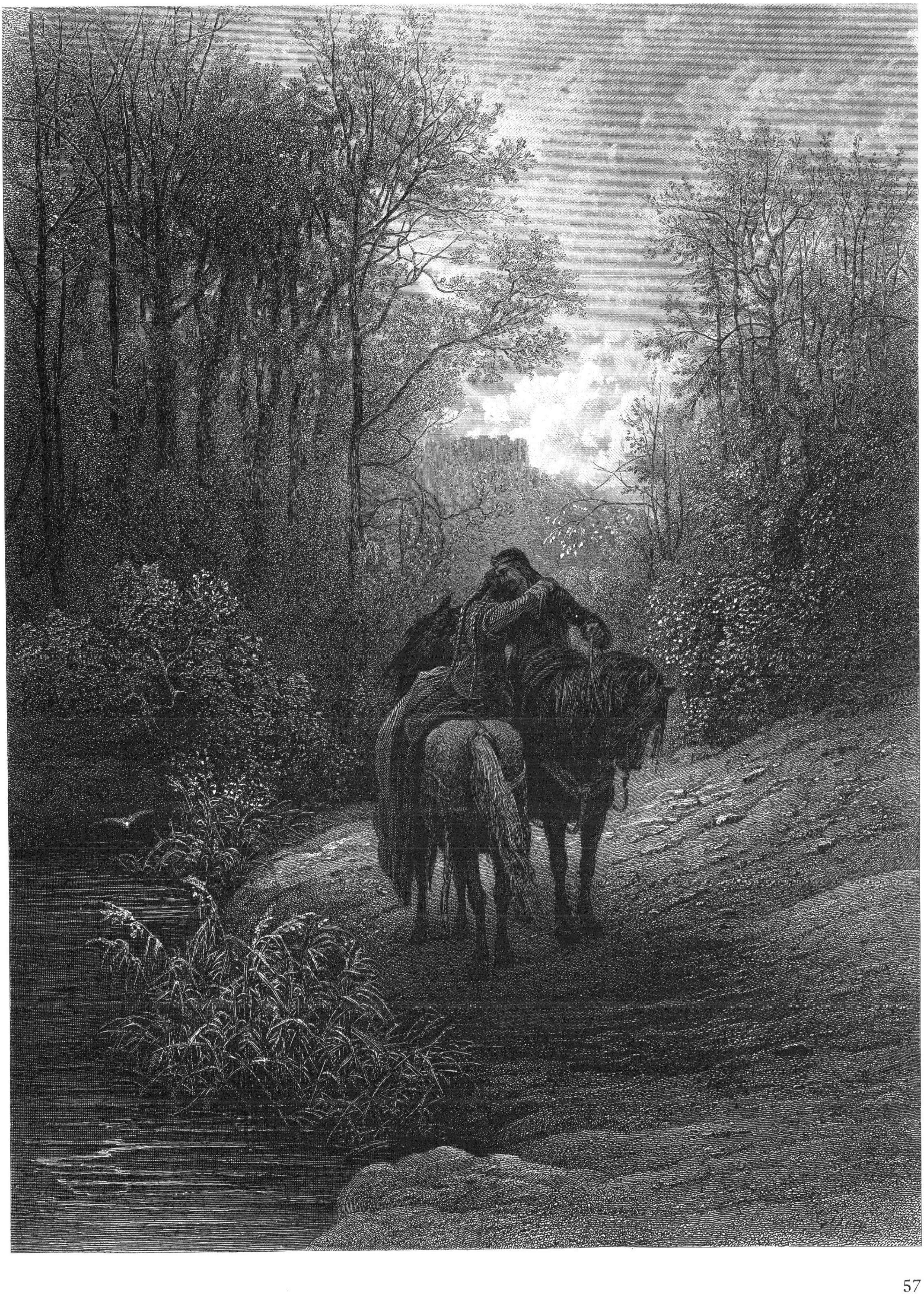

# Plate XXIX

After Guinevere has convinced Lancelot to return to his own country, Arthur and his more loyal knights pursue him, believing the Queen to be with him. Mordred, taking advantage of the havoc created by the lovers' flight and Arthur's absence, usurps the kingdom and joins forces with the heathens who have invaded the realm. Unknown to anyone but Lancelot, Guinevere has traveled alone to a nunnery at Almesbury, to seek refuge and perform penance.

[S]he to Almesbury
Fled all night long by glimmering waste and weald,
And heard the Spirits of the waste and weald
Moan as she fled, or thought she heard them moan:
And in herself she moan'd too late, too late!
Till in the cold wind that foreruns the morn,
A blot in heaven, the Raven, flying high,
Croak'd, and she thought "he spies a field of death;
For now the Heathen of the Northern Sea,
Lured by the crimes and frailties of the court,
Begin to slay the folk, and spoil the land."
And when she came to Almesbury she spake
There to the nuns, and said, "mine enemies
Pursue me, but, O peaceful Sisterhood,
Receive, and yield me sanctuary, nor ask
Her name, to whom ye yield it, till her time
To tell you:" and her beauty, grace and power,
Wrought as a charm upon them, and they spared
To ask it. (127–145)

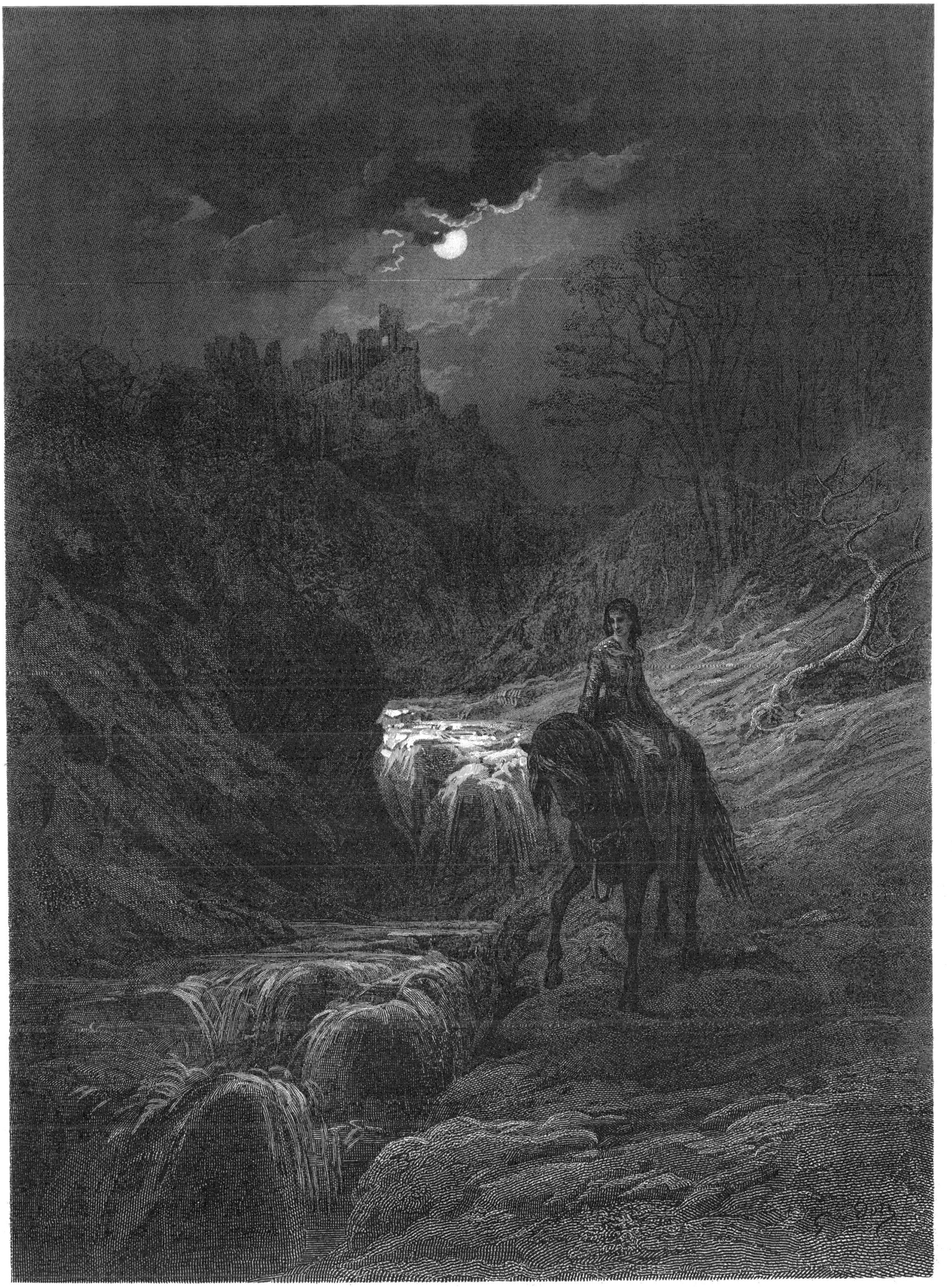

# Plate XXX

Accepted by the nuns, Guinevere stays at Almesbury. Despite their acceptance, however, Guinevere remains aloof from all society, taking care not to reveal her identity or the true cause of her grief. Guinevere's only comfort is the company of a young novice, "Who pleased her with a babbling heedlessness / Which often lured her from herself." One evening through the child's idle chatter, Guinevere learns that Mordred has usurped the kingdom and that Arthur is waging war against Lancelot. She then realizes the true cost of her adulterous love, and in her remorse, she asks the maid to "Sing, and unbind my heart that I may weep." Ignorant of whom she is addressing, the girl tries to comfort her by suggesting Guinevere compare her sorrows to those of the King.

"Ah sweet lady, the King's grief
For his own self, and his own Queen, and realm,
Must needs be thrice as great as any of ours.
For me, I thank the saints, I am not great.
For if there ever come a grief to me
I cry my cry in silence, and have done:
None knows it, and my tears have brought me good:
But even were the griefs of little ones
As great as those of great ones, yet this grief
Is added to the griefs the great must bear,
That howsoever much they may desire
Silence, they cannot weep behind a cloud:
As even here they talk at Almesbury
About the good King and his wicked Queen,
And were I such a King with such a Queen,
Well might I wish to veil her wickedness,
But were I such a King, it could not be." (196–212)

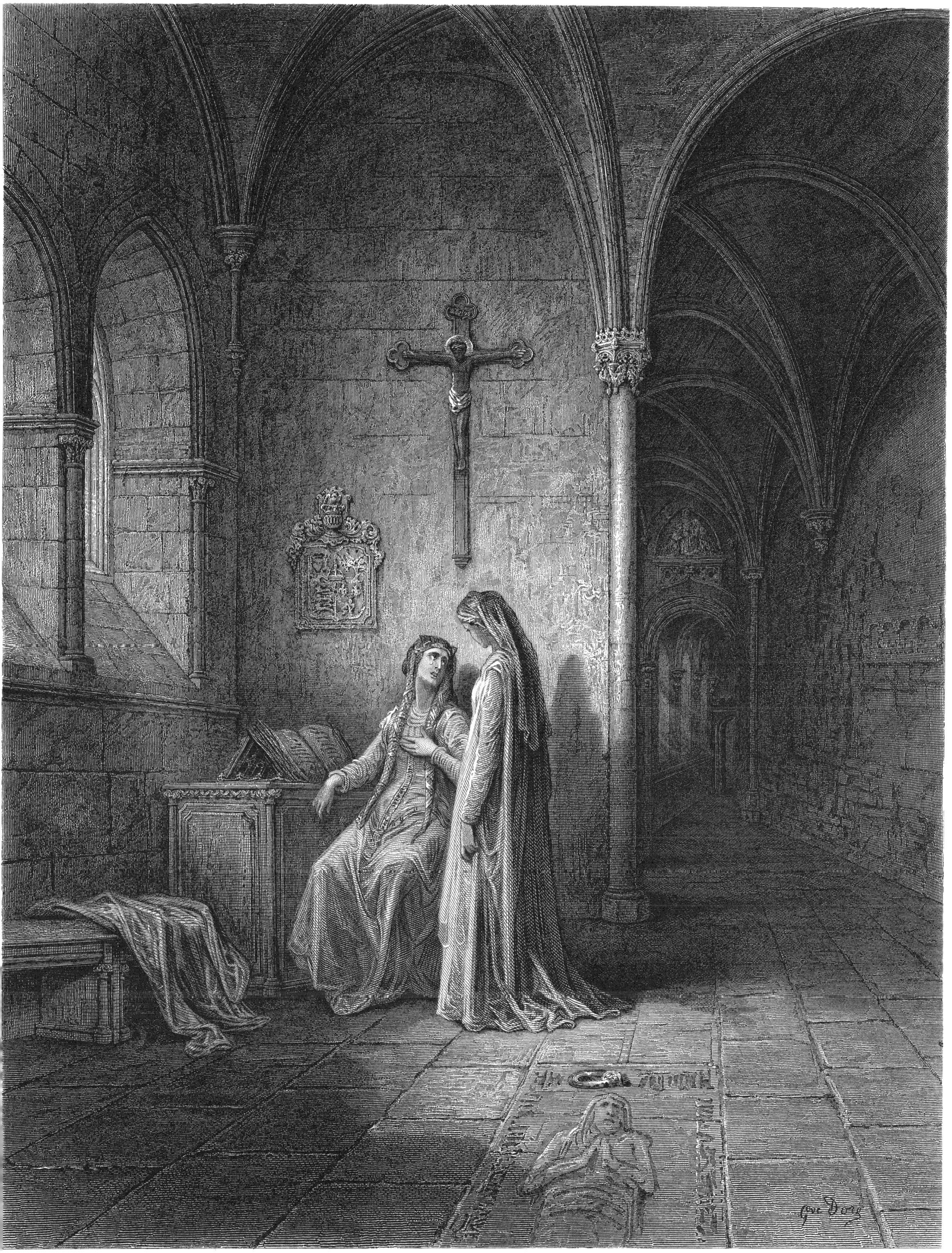

# Plate XXXI

Guinevere is tortured by the maid's comments, and argues that her grief is one that must be felt by everyone in the realm. The girl agrees, claiming that women should feel the grief even more keenly, since all the confusion and turmoil in the kingdom has been caused by a woman's disloyalty.

> Then to her own sad heart mutter'd the Queen,
> "Will the child kill me with her innocent talk?"
> But openly she answer'd, "must not I,
> If this false traitor have displaced his lord,
> Grieve with the common grief of all the realm?"
> "Yea," said the maid, "this is all woman's grief,
> That *she* is a woman, whose disloyal life
> Hath wrought confusion in the Table Round
> Which good King Arthur founded, years ago,
> With signs and miracles and wonders, there
> At Camelot, ere the coming of the Queen." (213–223)

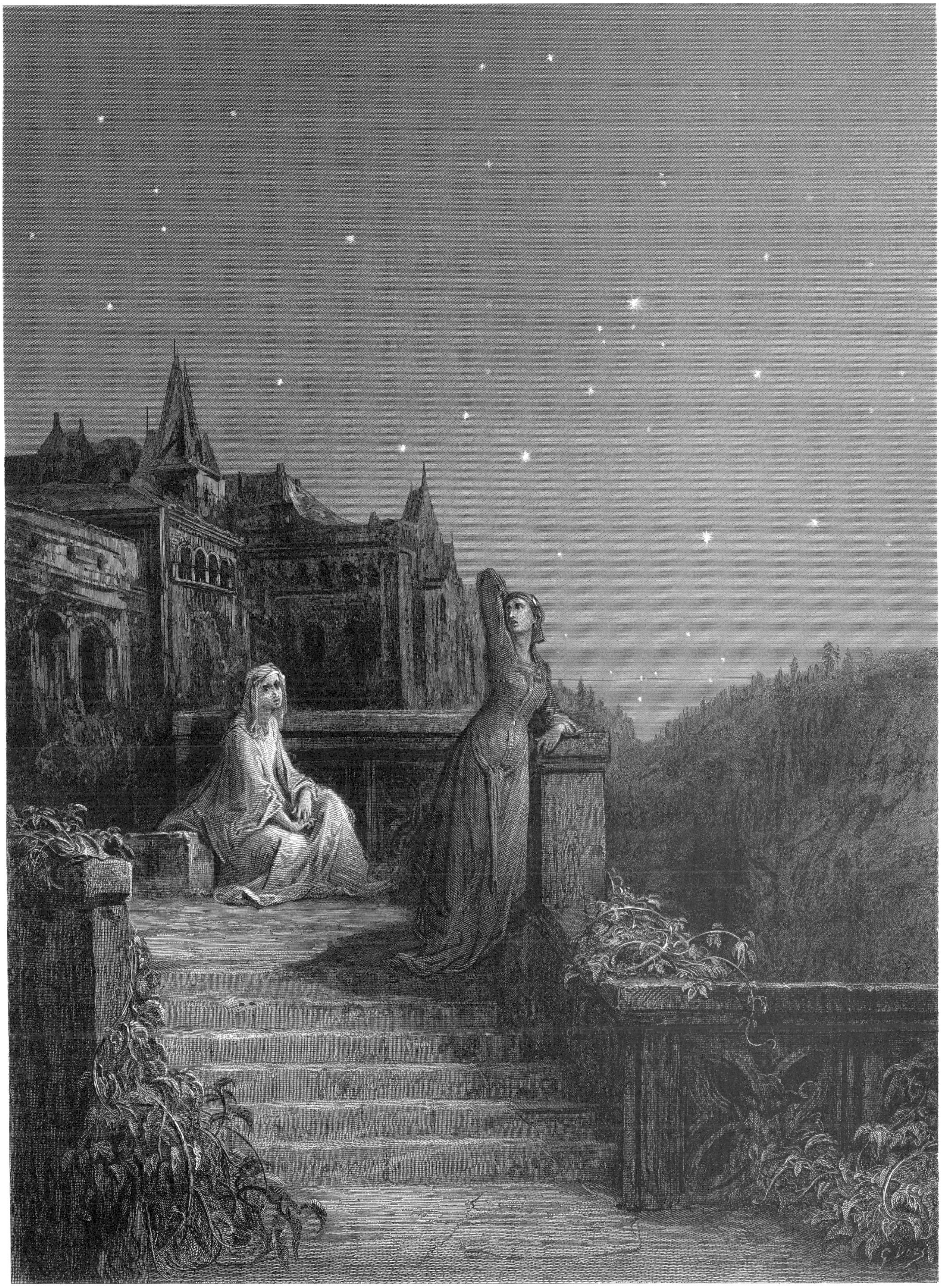

# Plate XXXII

Guinevere continues to listen to her young companion, painfully aware that she is the wicked Queen the girl speaks of. To divert attention from her own reaction to the girl's prattle, Guinevere asks how she could possibly know anything about Arthur and the Round Table, shut up as she is in a nunnery. The novice then tells Guinevere that her father was once a knight of the Round Table, and that he himself had seen the signs and wonders that portended the founding of the Round Table.

[A]nd he said
That as he rode, an hour or maybe twain
After the sunset, down the coast, he heard
Strange music, and he paused and turning—there,
All down the lonely coast of Lyonnesse,
Each with a beacon-star upon his head,
And with a wild sea-light about his feet,
He saw them—headland after headland flame
Far on into the rich heart of the west:
And in the light the white mermaiden swam,
And strong man-breasted things stood from the sea,
And sent a deep sea-voice thro' all the land,
To which the little elves of chasm and cleft
Made answer, sounding like a distant horn.
So said my father—yea, and furthermore,
Next morning, while he past the dim-lit woods,
Himself beheld three spirits mad with joy
Come dashing down on a tall wayside flower,
That shook beneath them, as the thistle shakes
When three gray linnets wrangle for the seed." (236–255)

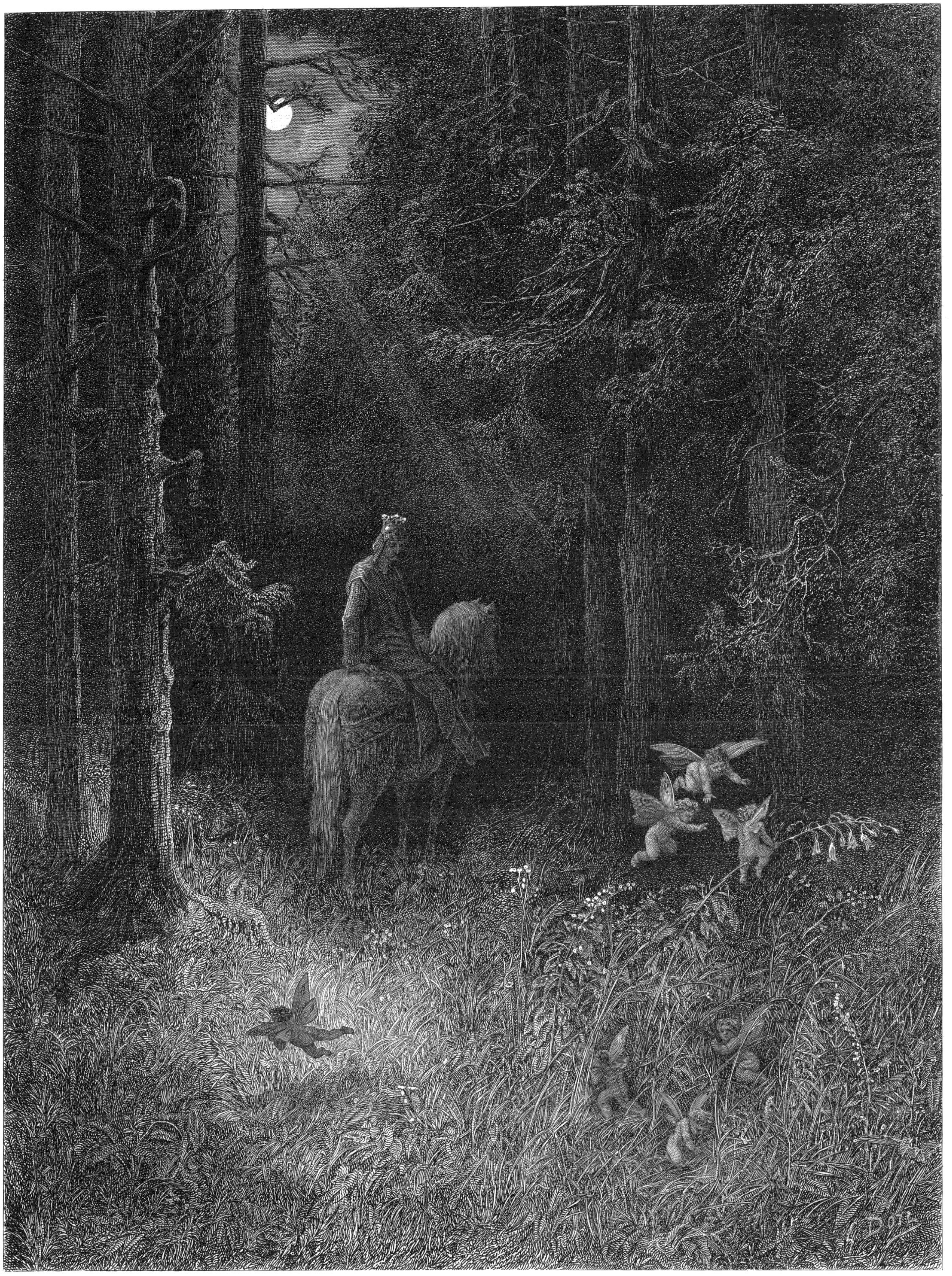

# Plate XXXIII

The novice continues to tell Guinevere all the miracles her father witnessed, before the Queen came to Camelot and destroyed the new ideals that Arthur had instilled in the kingdom.

And still at evenings on before his horse
The flickering fairy-circle wheel'd and broke
Flying, and link'd again, and wheel'd and broke
Flying, for all the land was full of life.
And when at last he came to Camelot,
A wreath of airy dancers hand-in-hand
Swung round the lighted lantern of the hall;
And in the hall itself was such a feast
As never man had dream'd; for every knight
Had whatsoever meat he long'd for served
By hands unseen; and even as he said
Down in the cellars merry bloated things
Shoulder'd the spigot, straddling on the butts
While the wine ran: so glad were the spirits and men
Before the coming of the sinful Queen." (256–270)

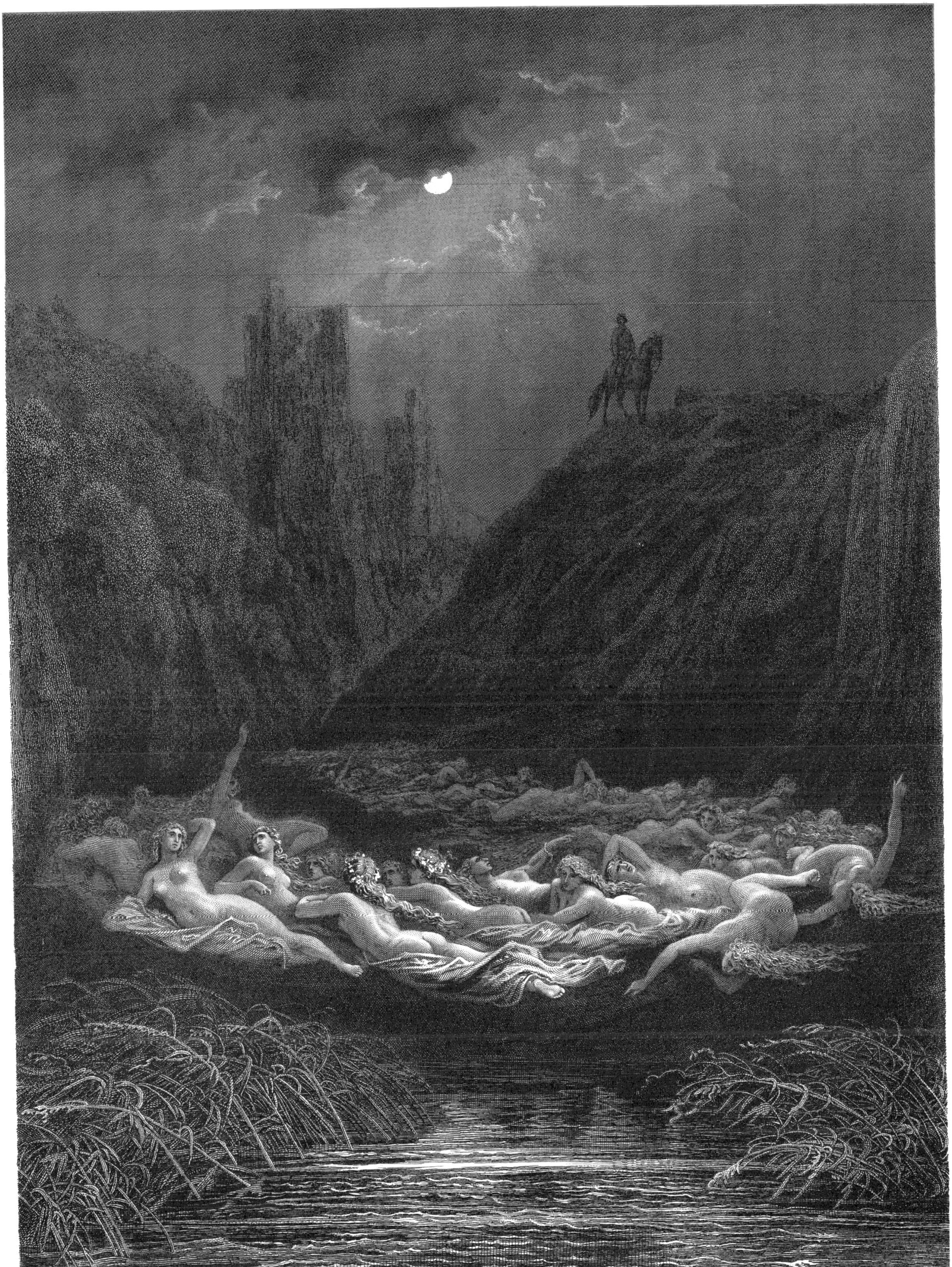

# Plate XXXIV

Embittered by the suggestion that such happiness and content reigned at Camelot until her arrival, Guinevere criticizes the knights for their lack of foresight. Was there no one, she asks, who could predict what was now happening? The novice answers that there was one prophet, a bard, who was devoted to Arthur and his cause, and who would brook no criticism of the King—even though no one knew "from whence he came." She then repeats the story of Arthur's coming and the bard's vision of his future.

"There came a day as still as Heaven, and then
They found a naked child upon the sands
Of dark Dundagil by the Cornish sea;
And that was Arthur; and they foster'd him
Till he by miracle was approven king:
And that his grave should be a mystery
From all men, like his birth; and could he find
A woman in her womanhood as great
As he was in his manhood, then, he sang,
The twain together well might change the world.
And even in the middle of his song
He falter'd, and his hand fell from the harp,
And pale he turn'd, and reel'd, and would have fall'n,
. . . nor would he tell
His vision; but what doubt that he foresaw
This evil work of Lancelot and the Queen?" (292–307)

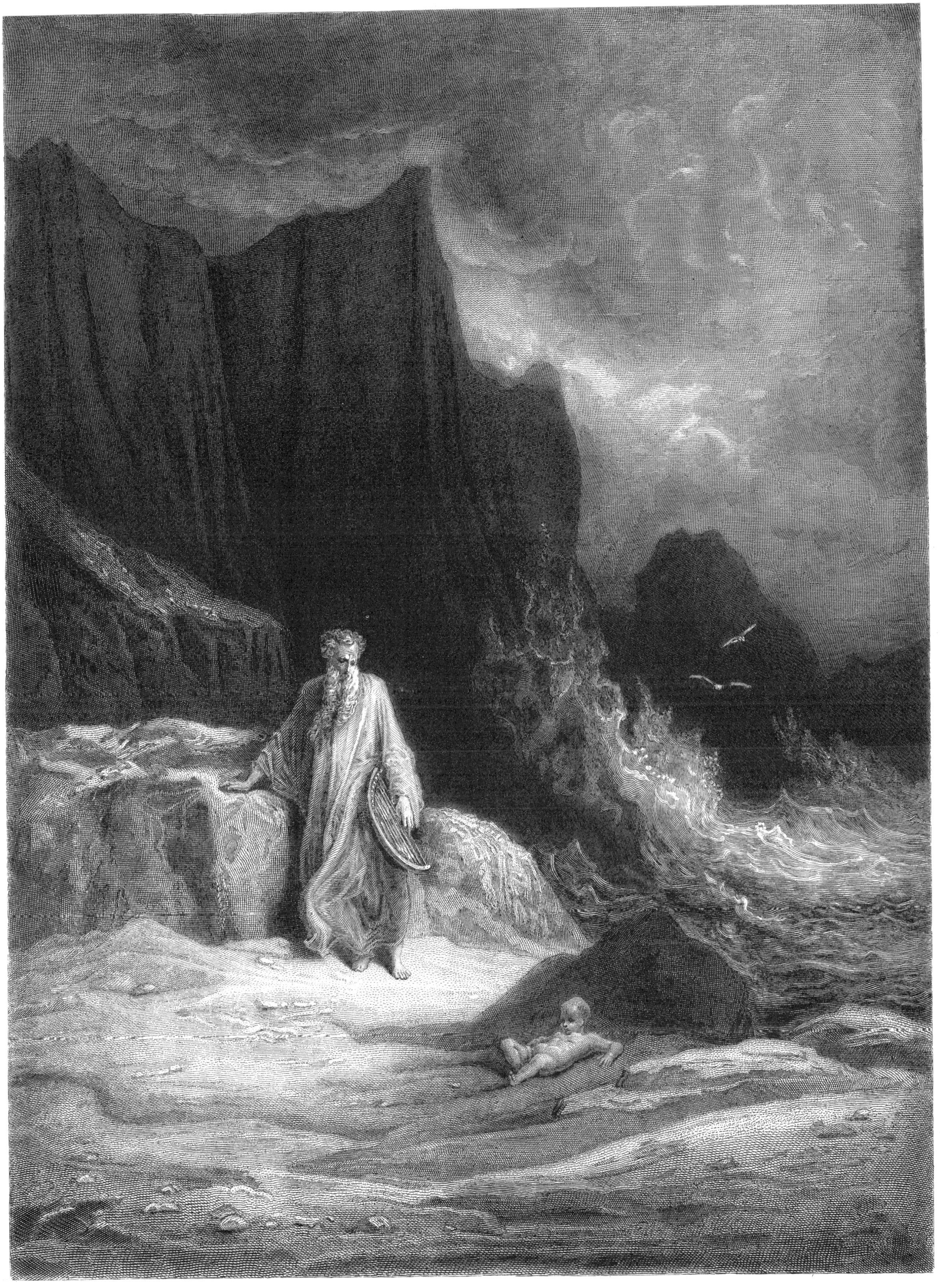

# Plate XXXV

The Queen now believes the nuns know who she is and that they have sent the novice to torture her with her stories. In a burst of anger she dismisses the girl. Left alone, Guinevere realizes that it is her own guilt that makes her so suspicious of a child. She resolves to repent of her sins with Lancelot and never to think of him again. But even as she makes her resolution, her thoughts turn to her first happy days with Lancelot, before she was married to Arthur.

Her memory from old habit of the mind
Went slipping back upon the golden days
In which she saw him first, when Lancelot came,
Reputed the best knight and goodliest man,
Ambassador, to lead her to his lord
Arthur, and led her forth, and far ahead
Of his and her retinue moving, they,
Rapt in sweet talk or lively, all on love
And sport and tilts and pleasure, (for the time
Was maytime, and as yet no sin was dream'd,)
Rode under groves that look'd a paradise
Of blossom, over sheets of hyacinth
That seem'd the heavens upbreaking thro' the earth. (378–390)

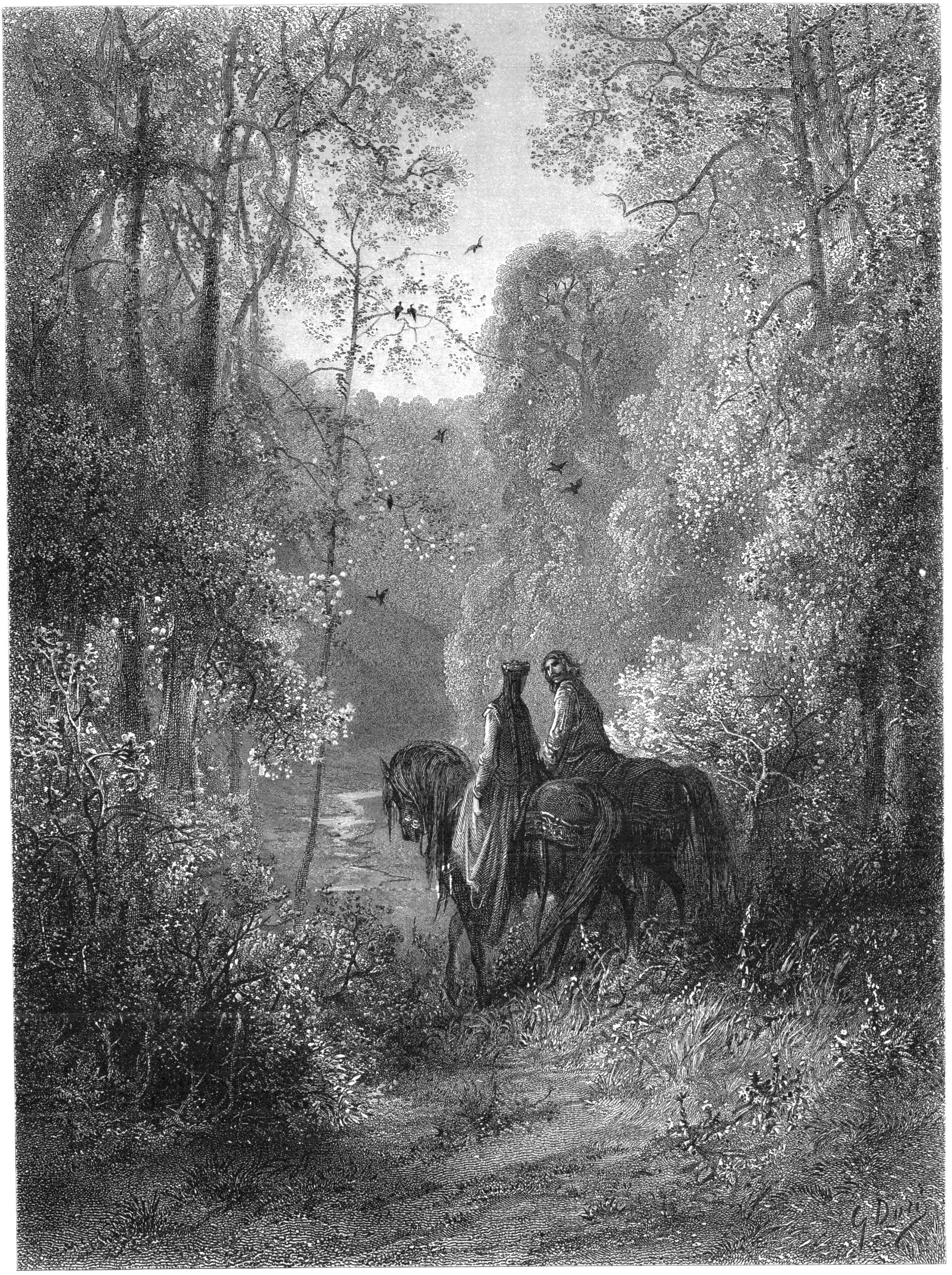

# Plate XXXVI

As Guinevere reminisces, King Arthur arrives; at the sound of his footsteps the Queen falls to the floor and remains there with her face hidden. He has come, he tells her, not to punish her, nor to take her away, but to tell her what has happened as a result of her sin. The kingdom has been split into factions, and lawlessness reigns as it did in the days before the Round Table. Even though all of these evils have been loosed due to her infidelity, Arthur forgives her, and declares that he still loves her, even though he cannot take her back as his Queen.

> "I did not come to curse thee, Guinevere,
> I, whose vast pity almost makes me die
> To see thee, laying there thy golden head,
> My pride in happier summers, at my feet. . . .
> [A]ll is past, the sin is sinn'd, and I,
> Lo! I forgive thee, as Eternal God
> Forgives: do thou for thine own soul the rest.
> But how to take last leave of all I loved? . . .
> Let no man dream but that I love thee still. . . .
> And while she grovell'd at his feet,
> She felt the King's breath wander o'er her neck
> And, in the darkness o'er her fallen head,
> Perceived the waving of his hands that blest. (531–581)

When Arthur leaves, Guinevere realizes that she has really loved him all along, and that her love for Lancelot was only a desire for "warmth and colour." Truly repentant and hopeful of Arthur's promise that they may one day meet in heaven as husband and wife, Guinevere lives the remainder of her days in the convent.

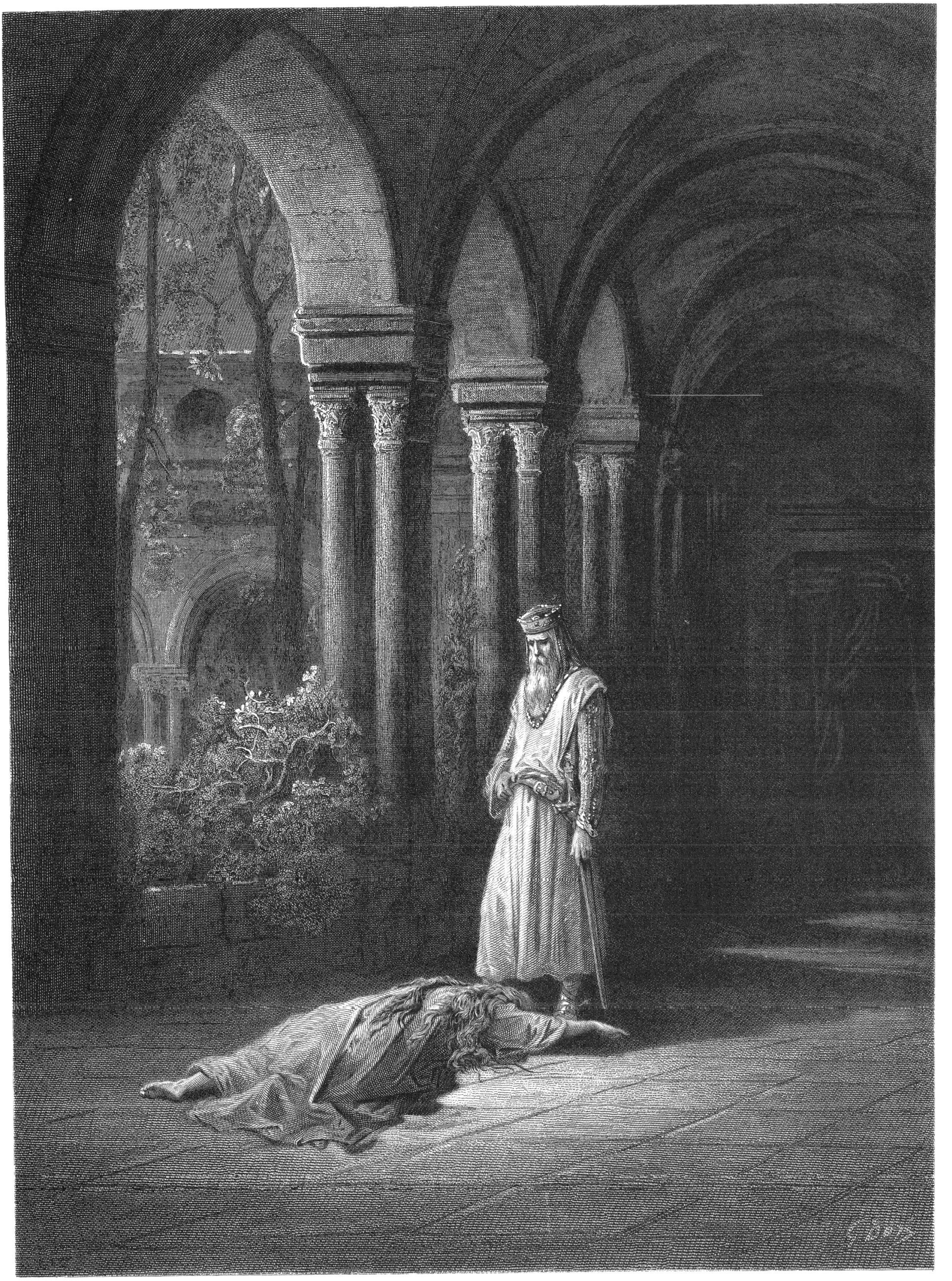